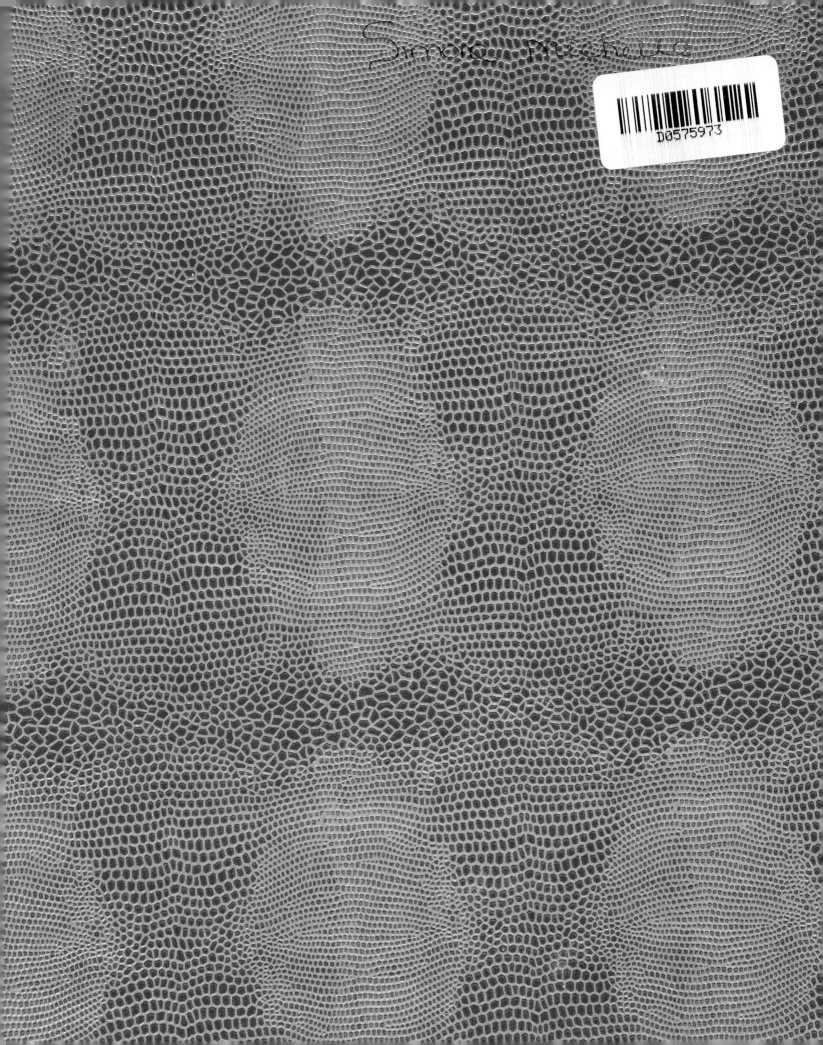

★ HOT ★
COUNTRY
STARS

PUBLICATIONS INTERNATIONAL, LTD.

Louis Weber, C.E.O.
Publications International, Ltd.
7373 N. Cicero Avenue
Lincolnwood, Illinois 60646

Manufactured in U.S.A.

8 7 6 5 4 3 2 1

ISBN 1-56173-729-1

Contributing writers:

MICHAEL McCALL is a Nashville-based country music and entertainment writer whose credits include a biography of Garth Brooks and articles in *US* and *Billboard.* He served as music critic and feature writer for the *Nashville Banner* for seven years, and he is currently a columnist for the *Nashville Scene.*

JANET WILLIAMS, a Nashville resident, has closely followed the country music scene by interviewing artists and writing features in her role as the associate editor of the Country Music Association's magazine *Close Up.* Previously, she served as an associate producer of USA Network's *Night Flight.*

CONTENTS

As the country music industry steps forcefully toward the 21st century, the executives who make the decisions and the artists who create the sounds still like to think of themselves as one big, entertaining family. When Capitol-Nashville Records tossed a party in September 1991 to celebrate an unprecedented achievement in the annals of American culture, they invited the entire Nashville musical and political community to the join the celebration. The event marked the debut of Garth Brooks's third album, *Ropin' the Wind*, which had been declared the number-one album in the country its first week out of the chute. It was a first for country music, and a clarion blast suggesting that country musicians were ready to rise above the second-level status they'd endured since Elvis Presley began shaking his hips and Bill Haley set America rockin' around the clock.

Garth Brooks wasn't the only listing on the *Billboard* magazine charts that suggested a new dawn had arrived. Other names taking up space on the top albums chart included Reba McEntire, George Strait, Randy Travis, Alan Jackson, Clint Black, Travis Tritt, Vince Gill, Trisha Yearwood, Ricky Van Shelton, Pam Tillis, and others. More than 30 country artists were listed among the hottest 200 albums, an unheard of statistic just a few years earlier.

Country album sales have skyrocketed. Capitol-Nashville (which changed its name to Liberty Records in January 1992) sold more than 20 million albums in 1991, an increase of more than 1,000 percent from five years earlier. MCA tallied more than $15 million in sales of country albums in 1991, a 50 percent increase over the previous 12 months. In all, 30 country music albums achieved gold or platinum certification in 1991 for sales of 500,000 or one million, respectively.

Dominant forces in the new country music include Randy Travis (*above*) and Garth Brooks (*above, right*).

Other success indicators abound. Country music replaced top-40 as the third most popular radio format in America, coming in just behind adult contemporary stations and news-talk formats. Giant Records and Elektra Records opened new Nashville division offices in 1991 and 1992, hoping to take part in the new country sales bonanza. They were preceded by other companies—Arista, Atlantic, Curb, Capricorn—that invested in the future of country music by establishing new division offices in Nashville.

The good news stretched beyond record sales and the achievement of record companies. Country talent bookings for concerts, for television, and for commercial endorsements grew in 1991. While the rest of the music industry was fighting a downward trend in concert sales brought on by an economic recession, many country artists were playing to packed houses and larger-than-ever audiences. In 1991,

Fan Fair, an annual five-day extravaganza of music and autograph signing held at the Tennessee State Fairgrounds each June, sold out its 24,000 tickets two weeks in advance for the first time in its 20-year history.

The enthusiasm swept into the television industry as well. In an attempt to lift its Sunday night ratings, NBC debuted *Hot Country Nights* in late 1991, making country the only musical genre to have its own variety show. The program immediately increased NBC's Sunday night audience.

Country's sudden leap into the mainstream of American entertainment actually was a decade in the making. In the late 1970s, country enjoyed a short-lived revival thanks to the success of the movie *Urban Cowboy*. At the time, Nashville reacted by trying to make country music sound more like pop music, replacing fiddles with string sections and steel guitars with synthesizers. For some, it stole the soul out of country music and loosened the bedrock of honest, straightforward lyrics and simple, unpretentious arrangements

that the sound was built upon. Sales soon reversed and started to plunge.

In 1981, Ricky Skaggs and George Strait offered a different option. The two surprised the country industry by attracting young fans with a back-to-basics sound that drew directly from older, traditional elements of the music. Skaggs had roots in the bluegrass and mountain music of the Southeast; Strait originally cut his heels playing swing and honky tonk tunes in the Southwest. Both stayed true to their heritage, and both are now credited with putting Nashville back on track. Others followed: The Judds and Reba McEntire in 1984, Randy Travis and Dwight Yoakam in 1986, then Ricky Van Shelton and Patty Loveless, then Clint Black, Alan Jackson, and Garth Brooks.

Together, this extraordinary fusion of young talent, updated traditions, and new fans has taken country music to new heights. This notable success has revived a joke credited to country music legend Chet Atkins. "People used to ask me, 'What's the Nashville Sound?'" Atkins drawled. "I'd just reach in my pocket and jingle some coins. 'Hear that,' I'd say, 'that's the Nashville Sound.' It's the sound of money."

Millions of fans are devoted to exciting performers the caliber of Reba McEntire (*above*), Ricky Van Shelton (*left*), and Alan Jackson (*below*).

"Put Yourself in My Shoes"—that was the song Clint Black was singing in October of 1990. For aspiring singers who would gladly do just that, filling those shoes (or in Clint's case, boots) would mean losing every bit of anonymity. When his debut single, "A Better Man," exploded onto the country charts in May 1989, Clint Patrick Black stepped into a world where frenzied fans will stop at nothing to get a glimpse of their idols, a prized autograph, or more. Requests for locks of his hair have become routine for Black, while one zealous admirer handed him some nail clippers and asked for a few of his fingernail clippings.

Both pages: Clint Black needed just two years to become a dominant force in country music, and one of its most popular stars. His concert at New York City's Radio City Music Hall was a hot-ticket sellout. Although he grew up in Houston and calls that city home, Black was actually born in New Jersey.

The youngest of four sons born to G.A. and Ann Black, country boy Clint was actually born in New Jersey, where his father was working on a pipeline. His accent and cowboy hat are the result of being raised in Texas, however, which he considers home. When Black was a teenager, his parents recognized his musical abilities and encouraged him to cultivate his talents. He took their advice and was playing guitar, bass, and harmonica by the time he was 15.

The aspiring singer began performing at his parents' backyard barbecues. He enjoyed his barbeque serenades so much that he made the rounds of nearby parks, going from picnic table to picnic table singing to anybody who would listen. He also played bass and sang harmony in brother Kevin's band. Except for brief stints as an ironworker, bait cutter, and fishing guide, Black has spent most of his life performing.

With the help of a family friend, he landed a gig at Houston's Benton Springs Club in 1981. Armed with his acoustic guitar, the handsome Texan lived a hand-to-mouth existence on the rowdy Houston club circuit for the next six years, performing a mix of original tunes and songs by such country favorites as Merle Haggard. During one of those engagements, he met song-

writer Hayden Nicholas, who became his most frequent collaborator. After the two began writing songs together, Black took steps to get a record deal. Previously unable to afford studio time to put a tape together, the determined singer found the solution in his new friend's garage, which contained an eight-track home recording studio.

Through the efforts of local promotion man Sammy Alfano, a finished demo tape made its way into the hands of Bill Ham, manager of the rock band ZZ Top. Ham loved country music and was looking for a country artist to manage. Struck by the honesty of his lyrics and Black's distinctive vocals, Ham found just what he'd been looking for. "When I met my manager, that's when I consider I got my big break," Black told *CMA Close-Up* magazine.

Shortly after hooking up with Ham, Black met Joe Galante, then head of RCA Records' Nashville division. Clint had strolled into his office in Music City and played four demos. Impressed with the confident young singer, Galante agreed to fly to Houston to see him perform. "He seemed warm and caring," Galante told *USA Today*, "but he looked like he could be a little devilish. There's a glint in his eye. But in his music he's also bringing across serious thoughts." The trip to Houston paid off for both parties because Galante signed Black to an eight album contract.

Almost immediately, Black began working on a debut album and mapping out a career plan. His proficiency at songwriting was tested as he produced almost 50 song tapes. Each made the rounds of his preproduction team before nine were finally selected

Success has brought Black many grand moments, but he may never have been happier than when he appeared at a yellow-ribbon party with country-music legend Gene Autry.

Opposite: Long an avowed bachelor, Black made headlines in October 1991, when he married actress Lisa Hartman. The couple exchanged vows in a simple, private ceremony at Black's farm outside Houston.

as album material for his debut release, *Killin' Time.*

When the video of his first single, "A Better Man," was released in May 1989, Black became an instant hit. Female fans were attracted to his rugged good looks and the way he was poured into his Wrangler jeans. Suddenly, he was a country music sex symbol, and the industry began to take notice of what all the fireworks were about. Buck Owens quipped, "To me [Clint's] the kind of guy you'd want to take home to meet your father if you could trust your mother!"

"A Better Man" also put the hat-wearing hunk into the record books when it became the first debut single by a new male country artist to reach number one since the trade publication *Radio & Records* has been keeping charts. By the time Black released the much-heralded *Killin' Time*, fans were clamoring for more of his authentic-sounding country songs in traditional honky tonk arrangements. He obliged with the title cut off the album, which became another number-one single. Black exhibited confidence in the songs on his album, probably because he used his own band as backup rather than relying on Nashville session musicians. Though Music City has some of the finest session players in the country, recording with his own band guaranteed that the music in Black's concerts lived up to that on his album.

With just two singles, two videos, and one album to his credit, Black was honored with three Country Music Association Award nominations in October 1989. Black walked away with the Horizon Award, which is bestowed

on the performer who has advanced the farthest during the previous year.

As Clint's career began to barrel down the fast track, he found himself performing with K.T. Oslin to a sold-out crowd at Carnegie Hall in October 1989. Shortly thereafter, he debuted his next single, "Nobody's Home," on *The Tonight Show.* By the dawn of the new decade, "Nobody's Home" became Black's third number-one record in a row, resulting in some incredible trade-publication recognition. Both *Billboard* magazine and *Radio & Records* named "A Better Man" and "Killin' Time" the top two country singles of 1989.

As *Killin' Time* went platinum, Black added an American Music Award to his trophy collection when he was named new artist of the year.

He also earned two Grammy nominations, one for best vocal performance by a country male and the other for best country song ("A Better Man"), a nomination he shared with cowriter Hayden Nicholas.

When the nominations for the The Nashville Network's 1990 Music City News Awards were announced live on TNN's *Video Morning* program, Black was on the list three times. He was nominated as male artist of the year and star of tomorrow, while *Killin' Time* was nominated for album of the year. When the trophies were handed out on June 4, 1990, Black was honored as the star of tomorrow, and his carefully selected collection of tunes was named album of the year.

During the 1991 CMA Awards, Black shared the stage with the ageless King of the Cowboys, Roy Rogers. The audience was thrilled when the pair teamed up to sing "Hold on Pardner."

Black's trophy case soon began to bulge, because the young Texan was also honored at the Academy of Country Music Awards that year. Outfitted in his trademark black Stetson hat, blue jeans, and a tuxedo jacket, Clint picked up four awards: He was named the year's top male vocalist and best new male vocalist; and *Killin' Time* was named album of the year while the title cut won as single of the year.

Capping off his incredible year of awards, chart-busting records, and industry accolades, Black released two more consecutive number-one singles, "Walking Away" and "Nothing's New." Clint was the first artist in any music format to release five consecutive number-one records from a debut album, according to *Radio & Records.*

Clint charted another course of awards and acclaim with the release of "Put Yourself in My Shoes," the title single from his second album. On October 9, 1990, he won the CMA Award for male vocalist of the year. He was also the first recipient of the Nashville Songwriters Association International Songwriter/Artist of the Year award. The album *Put Yourself in My Shoes* was received just as enthusiastically as its predecessor. Released in November of 1990, it was certified platinum that same month.

With his newfound clout, Clint decided to record a tune with the legendary King of the Cowboys, Roy Rogers. The lookalike singers teamed up for a video to accompany their

"Hold on Pardner" duet, which they performed at the 1991 CMA Awards.

Maintaining a nonstop touring schedule, Black seemed dedicated only to his career. He told numerous journalists throughout 1989 and 1990 that settling down and getting married was not in his immediate future. That attitude changed when he met actress Lisa Hartman following a New Year's Eve performance in 1991. Accompanied by her mother, Hartman came backstage following his show. "There were about 200 people backstage that night," Black recalled for *People* magazine. "But with those beautiful blue eyes, she stood out in the crowd."

The boyish king of country music and the sultry prime-time soap siren found they had a lot in common. Both grew up in Houston, neither had ever been married, and each professed no desire to do so—until they met, that is. Despite the difficulties of dating because of conflicting schedules, the romance blossomed. They chose to keep their relationship out of the public eye and surprised members of Nashville's music community when they announced their engagement at the 1991 ASCAP Country Songwriter Awards in late September. It was a short engagement. They were married on October 20, 1991, at Black's 180-acre farm outside Houston. They kept the ceremony private, inviting only about 30 family members. The only uninvited onlookers included ten horses, a herd of Brahma cattle, and a donkey who watched them exchange vows from the stable door. Black designed their wedding bands and wrote their vows.

Confident and in control, Clint Black is destined for a long career in country music, primarily because of his healthy attitude. He's serious about music and thinks of his writing and performing not only as his profession but also as a craft. "I don't look on this as a party," he disclosed to the *Boston Globe*. "That's where [famous performers of the past] made their mistake. And when people come to your show, you have to remember they're celebrating, so it's natural for them to say, 'Hey, have a drink.' But too much of that can kill you."

Confident and level-headed, Black is firmly in control of his life and career. In his rare moments of leisure, he enjoys spending time with his family.

Garth Brooks has set a new standard for country music success. In an unprecendented feat for a country artist, Garth's third album, *Ropin' the Wind*, reached the number-one spot music charts the release. Only two performers have top spot on the pop Cash in 1969 and

on *Billboard*'s pop first week of its previous country ever reached the charts—Johnny Kenny Rogers in

1980, and they did so only after weeks of steady sales. Brooks's album, which was released in September 1991, started out at the top.

Both pages: Garth Brooks has plenty to smile about—and sing about—these days. By early 1992, he had become America's hottest recording artist, and was handily outselling such established pop stars as Michael Jackson and U2.

Just as remarkable, *Ropin' the Wind* has continued to amaze the music industry with its endurance. Through the fall of 1991 and early 1992, it was the best-selling album in America, clinging to the pole position of the sales charts despite competition from pop music's biggest names. *Use Your Illusion II* by Guns N' Roses dislodged *Ropin' the Wind* briefly, but, as soon as the rock band's initial blast of sales slacked off, the album by the self-described "chubby kid" from Oklahoma returned to number one. Brooks withstood challenges from rap star Hammer and rhythm-and-blues diva Mariah Carey before relinquishing his perch to Michael Jackson, whose high-profile *Dangerous* was the international super-

star's first album in four years. Within weeks, however, *Ropin' the Wind* booted *Dangerous* out of the cherished peak slot.

To the pop music industry, this brash country singer seemed to emerge from nowhere to capture the fancy of the American public. "What is a Garth Brooks?," pondered a member of the rock group Metallica, the act Brooks originally knocked off the top of the pop charts. While Garth insists that he's just a fun-loving regular guy playing the music that he loves, others maintain that he possesses the inner strength to follow his convictions. He's tackled subjects outside the conventions of Nashville and invested a wild-eyed energy into his performances that combines

The shadowy lighting and misty background are part of the dramatic setting of Brooks's "The Thunder Rolls" video, which was banned by The Nashville Network and Country Music Television because of its depiction of domestic violence.

the force and flash of rock 'n' roll with the lyrical substance and everyman humility of country music.

What exactly is a Garth Brooks? A native Oklahoman, he was the sixth and last child to join the clan of Troyal and Colleen Brooks. Brooks describes his mother as affectionate, lively, and quick to show her emotions. His father is low-key, stern, but big-hearted. Both had been married previously, and their children were brought together when Troyal and Colleen united. Then the couple had two children of their own, including Garth. Though the six children have three sets of parents, they're a close-knit family that doesn't care for the term half-brother or half-sister. Brooks's half-sister Betsy Smittle plays bass in his band, Stillwater. His brother Kelly travels with him as a tour accountant.

Brooks excelled at several sports while growing up in Yukon, Oklahoma, a tiny hamlet outside of Oklahoma City. He was the quarterback for the Yukon High School football team, and he was a decent student who was popular with both his peers and instructors. Though born into a musical family (his mother recorded for Capitol Records and starred on the *Ozark Mountain Jubilee* in the 1950s), Brooks didn't pick up a guitar until he was a junior in high school. After graduation, he attended Oklahoma State University on an athletic scholarship as a javelin thrower.

While in college, Brooks started performing in nightclubs. At first he performed solo, offering his interpretation of songs by such personal heroes as James Taylor and Dan Fogelberg.

Before long, he joined a band, mixing tunes by George Strait and Merle Haggard with those of the Georgia Satellites, Billy Joel, Bob Seger, and other rock bands.

In 1984, Brooks auditioned for Opryland USA and was invited to join the Nashville-based amusement park as a performer that summer. His parents feared he would quit college altogether, so they talked him out it; but they promised he would have their full support in chasing his musical dreams after he attained a college degree. In 1985, with a degree in advertising in hand, Brooks set out for Nashville and a country music career with his parents' support. He lasted 23 hours! A meeting with a music executive left him so discouraged that he returned to Oklahoma to assess his future.

Two years later, Brooks returned to Nashville, this time accompanied by his bride of one year, Sandy Mahl. The two had met when he ejected her from a nightclub where he was working as a bouncer. This time, Brooks had better luck in Nashville. Within days of his arrival, he was introduced to Bob Doyle, an executive at ASCAP (the American Society of Composers, Authors, and Publishers, which is a performing rights agency). Doyle's faith in Brooks's talent led him to leave ASCAP and form his own music publishing company, Major Bob Music, with Garth as his first client. A few months later, Doyle formed an artists' management company with publicist Pam Lewis. Just eight months after Garth arrived in Nashville, he signed a recording contract with Capitol Records.

When Capitol introduced him to Allen Reynolds, a record producer who had also worked with Kathy Mattea, Don Williams, and Crystal Gayle, Garth's approach to music began to take shape. Reynolds produced Brooks's 1989 debut album, *Garth Brooks*, and would later produce *No Fences* and *Ropin' the Wind*. It was Reynolds who suggested that Brooks stop singing ballads in the full-voiced, operatic style associated with Gary Morris or Lee Greenwood. The producer encouraged Brooks to relax and sing in a gentler, more natural manner. Reynolds's coaching later proved to be a key to Brooks's success in conveying the tender emotion of the ballads "If Tomorrow Never Comes" and "The Dance." Both songs have since become signature hits for the dynamic young entertainer.

Garth's debut album also included the hits "Not Counting You" and "Much Too Young (To Feel This Damn Old)," the latter about a rodeo cowboy, a recurring subject in Brooks's songs. Of the four hits from the first album, Brooks wrote or cowrote all but "The Dance." He has since continued to write about half of the songs on his albums.

Though his first album initially sold well for a debut, Brooks spent 1989 in the shadow of Clint Black, whose debut album sold a million copies in its first eight months. *Garth Brooks*, on the other hand, sold 500,000 copies in its first year. Garth received the news of that milestone on May 24, 1990, the fourth anniversary of his marriage. By then, "The Dance" was a major hit, and *Garth Brooks* sold another half-million copies in June.

Brooks holds a single rose during a performance of "Shameless," a song written by Billy Joel, who first saw Brooks perform the song on the nationally televised CMA Awards in October 1991. Joel later remarked, "It really knocked me out."

The sales of Brooks's albums have proliferated ever since. His second album, *No Fences*, sold 700,000 copies the first ten days it was in stores, thanks to the blockbuster hit "Friends in Low Places." The first week of October 1990, both the first and second album crossed the million mark in sales. That same week, Brooks reached two more milestones: He became the 65th member of the Grand Ole Opry, and he was the most-nominated artist at the 1990 Country Music Association Awards. Of his five nominations, Brooks won the award for video of the year for "The Dance" and the Horizon Award, given to the artist who had achieved the greatest career strides during the year.

Since then, Brooks has become country music's biggest seller as well as a major award winner. The *No Fences* collection remained the number-one country album until the fall of 1991, when it slipped to number two as *Ropin' the Wind* took the top spot. By the start of 1992, his debut album had sold more than four million, while both *No Fences* and *Ropin' the Wind* topped the six million mark. The leading music industry trade magazines, *Billboard* and *Radio & Records*, selected Brooks as male country artist of the year. He walked away with six Academy of Country Music Awards in April 1991 and four Country Music Association Awards the following October, claiming the prestigious Entertainer of the Year honors at both pageants. In 1992, he won American Music awards for best male country artist, best country single for "The Thunder Rolls," and best country album for *No Fences*.

Brooks made his acting debut on the November 2, 1991 episode of NBC-TV's *Empty Nest*, in which he played himself. Here Brooks hobnobs with costars Kristy McNichol, Park Overall, and Richard Mulligan.

Opposite: As in his music, Brooks blends the traditional and the flamboyant in his stage attire. He wears the standard cowboy singer's uniform of 10-gallon hat and Wrangler jeans, then tops it off with shirts of outrageous patterns and colors.

In concert, Garth Brooks's onstage enthusiasm pumps the crowd into hysterics. He'll do almost anything for a response: He'll sprint across the stage, dangle from a ladder, swing from ropes, and douse himself with water. Mainstream American audiences were introduced to his maniacal performing style when the dynamic singer was featured in a prime-time NBC-TV special titled *This Is Garth Brooks* in January 1992. (He has also appeared as himself in an episode of the NBC sitcom *Empty Nest*.)

Brooks seems just as personally motivated to make his videos enjoyable and effective for audiences. He fought with the director of "The Dance" video over the final edit, finally getting his way; he vetoed a video of "Friends in Low Places" before it could be televised because he didn't like how it turned out; and the "The Thunder Rolls" video was banned from The Nashville Network and Country Music Television (both owned by Gaylord Communications) because of its bleak depiction of domestic violence. Mixed feelings about the video for "The Thunder Rolls" existed in the country music industry; despite its ban, the video was honored as the best of the year by the Country Music Association.

As for the future, Brooks promises to keep taking chances and coming up with surprises. He also plans to be around awhile. "A big word for me is seven letters, something George Jones and George Strait have been able to do—sustain," he said backstage after being named Entertainer of the Year by the CMA. "I want to be here a long time and not be a flash in the pan."

Kix Brooks and Ronnie Dunn exploded on the country music scene in 1991 with their debut album *Brand New Man*. The hard-edged honky tonk music on this album gave the illusion that the pair had been singing together a long time, but in reality they had known each other less than a year when their record was released.

Leon "Kix" Brooks, a native of Shreveport, Louisiana, had made quite a name for himself in Nashville as the songwriter behind several number-one records, including "Bobbie Sue" by the Oak Ridge Boys, "Who's Lonely Now" by Highway 101, and "Modern Day Romance" by the Nitty Gritty Dirt Band.

The natural camaraderie that exists between singing duo Kix Brooks (*left*) and Ronnie Dunn is evident whenever they perform. Dunn's easygoing manner is a perfect complement to his partner's more flamboyant style.

Although Brooks had established himself as a top tunesmith, he still dreamed of being a recording artist. He pitched himself as a singer to Tim DuBois, head of Arista Records in Nashville, who kept Brooks's demo tape on file.

Ronnie Dunn was a virtual unknown when he arrived in Nashville from Tulsa, Oklahoma. His only claim to fame was winning the nationwide 1990 Marlboro Talent Search. Part of the prize included some studio time with top Nashville producer and engineer Scott Hendricks. Hendricks recorded Dunn on tape and took the material over to DuBois, who, like most record executives, is always scouting for fresh talent.

DuBois was interested in both Kix Brooks and Ronnie Dunn. He quickly set up a meeting and, over an enchilada, suggested the two get together to write some songs. "He was real evasive, didn't say anything about what was going on," Ronnie recalls. "We thought maybe he was putting us together to write for Alan Jackson or somebody on the [Arista] label. We got together, wrote 'My Next Broken Heart,' and took it to him. He got through with the song and said, 'Y'all have got a deal.'" The two were enthusiastic about their recording contract with Arista, yet both remained wary, knowing that landing a deal didn't guarantee success.

A chemistry gradually developed between them as they started writing, recording, and performing together. Their first single, "Brand New Man," delivered a no-holds-barred honky tonk sound with a contemporary edge, and it soon hit the top of the country charts. Their follow-up single, "My Next Broken Heart," also went number one and was accompanied by a music video that showcased their individual personalities. Ronnie Dunn, all 6'4" of him, is lean, lanky, and laid-back, while Kix Brooks is a 6'2" dynamo with limitless energy. DuBois had seen each singer performing solo and realized that Brooks's animated performing style perfectly complemented Dunn's relaxed appearance.

Their musical influences range from country favorite Lefty Frizzell to rocker Glenn Frey. Brooks grew up down the street from singer Johnny Horton, whose wife Billie Jean had also been married to Hank Williams. "That was my first exposure to gold records and things like that, so I got the bug way back," he admits. Dunn's father performed in a country band and gave his young son his first taste of playing professionally. Ronnie still credits his father as his biggest musical influence. However, a career in music was not Dunn's initial choice. While taking instruction to become a Baptist minister, he was caught playing in honky tonks and was dismissed from his studies.

At the threshold of their promising careers, Kix Brooks and Ronnie Dunn are keeping in mind some advice from DuBois. "He said, 'Keep your boots on, stay in jeans, and keep it aggressive,'" says Ronnie. "That's just what we plan to do."

While Brooks (*right*) has been a fixture in Music City for years, Dunn is a relative newcomer to country music. Brooks finds his partner's enthusiasm refreshing.

In 1987, Mary-Chapin Carpenter decided she needed a tape of her music to sell in the clubs she played in and around Washington, D.C., so she recorded some songs in the low-tech basement studio of her longtime guitarist, John Jennings. The tape reached a CBS Records executive, who offered her a country record deal. With one new song added, the homemade tape became Carpenter's debut album, *Hometown Girl.*

She was far from a conventional country music prospect. Born in Princeton, New Jersey, and raised in Tokyo and Washington, D.C., Carpenter grew up in an upper-middle-class, urban household. Her father was an editor for *Life* magazine.

Mary-Chapin Carpenter performs "Down at the Twist and Shout" on the Country Music Association Awards program in October 1991. So infectious was her performance that she had audience member George Bush clapping along with her.

She attended Brown University and earned a degree in American Studies. Her musical tastes leaned toward rock 'n' roll and to such urban folk singers as Judy Collins and Peter, Paul, and Mary. The closest thing to a country album she heard while growing up were recordings by folk-music legend Woody Guthrie.

She did, however, spend an inordinate amount of time strumming her acoustic guitar in her bedroom while still in high school. Her father finally pressed her to try her songs at an open-mike night at a club down the street from the family home. She continued to perform through college, pursuing a music career more vigorously after graduation. Before long, she became a local D.C. favorite, winning several local awards, known as Whammies, at an annual gala hosted by the Washington Area Music Association.

Her commercial breakthrough came with *State of the Heart*, her second album for Columbia Records. "This time I had a real budget and a real amount of time to figure out what I wanted to say and how I wanted to say it," Carpenter explains. "It had more of a consistency, and it fulfilled me more artistically."

The album proved a better showcase for Carpenter's warm alto voice and her eclectic, hard-to-classify sound; in press material, she describes herself as a singer with an acoustic guitar fronting a rock 'n' roll band. Whatever she was, country radio took to her—as did listeners from all walks of life. The hits from *State of the Heart* include the sassy "How Do," the reflective "This Shirt,"

and a couple of hard-bitten songs about the end of a relationship, "Never Had It So Good" and "Quittin' Time." The album earned her an Academy of Country Music Award for top new female artist.

Her success continued with her third disc, *Shooting Straight in the Dark*, which, like the others, was coproduced by Carpenter and John Jennings. This time, the hits ranged from the harsh honesty of "You Win Again" to the exuberant "Down at the Twist and Shout," a Cajun dance tune recorded with a Louisiana band named Beausoleil. With *Shooting Straight in the Dark*, Carpenter continued to probe a wide emotional range with personal insight and keenly observed detail, revealing the folk influence on her music. Once again, she garnered critical praise while expanding her ever-growing group of fans.

Carpenter blends several musical styles and attracts fans from diverse backgrounds. Asked to identify her musical style, she once said, "I'm most comfortable saying I play acoustic guitar—and I front a rock 'n' roll band."

Carlene Carter springs from the most deeply rooted family tree in country music. A granddaughter of the legendary Maybelle Carter, Carlene's parents are June Carter Cash and Carl Smith. Country Music Hall of Fame member Johnny Cash is her stepfather, and Goldie Hill, a popular country singer during the 1950s, is her stepmother. Carter's extended family also includes stepsister Rosanne Cash and former brothers-in-law Marty Stuart and Rodney Crowell.

When Carlene chose to use the name Carter rather than Smith, she got her famous father's approval.

When Carlene Carter became the stepdaughter of Johnny Cash, her life changed dramatically.

Because there were no Carter males, she wanted to keep the name alive. Carl Smith has two sons to perpetuate his legacy, so he didn't object. "But," Carter laughs, "he sends me Christmas cards addressed to Carlene Smith Carter."

Considering her heritage, it's no surprise that Carter found herself with a hit country album in 1990 when Warner Bros. Records released *I Fell in*

Love. The energetic singer/songwriter garnered recognition and acclaim with the title track, which reached the number-three position on *Billboard*'s country chart.

But before finding success as a country performer, Carter ventured into other types of music. She began defining her own musical style while attending Nashville's Belmont College and landed her first record deal in 1978. Her quest for a sound she could call her own led her from her country roots to pop to rhythm and blues. Eventually, it led her to England. There she was married for a short time to rock 'n' roll singer Nick Lowe. (A bride at 15 and a mother at 16, Carter has been married and divorced three times.)

With five albums under her belt but no hits to her credit, Carter sought success as a songwriter. Such diverse acts as Emmylou Harris ("Easy from Now On"), the Doobie Brothers ("One Step Closer"), and the Go-Go's ("I'm the Only One") recorded her songs. She credits her mother, June Carter Cash, for the motivation to start writing. "Mama told me it was the best way to make a living. I didn't know how to start so I took a Tchaikovsky chord progression and wrote it out, and then I wrote a song to that chord progression with a different melody. That's how I figured out the process," Carter recalls.

In 1990, Carter became Nashville's unofficial homecoming queen when she not only returned to her country roots but also moved back to Music City. Three years earlier, she had joined the Carter Sisters for a London performance and then toured with the group for two years, a venture that was followed by a

Carter family album. The experience prepared her for her return to Nashville's music scene. Her adventurous life and her explorations of different musical styles definitely influenced the *I Fell in Love* album. Combining the bluegrass-inspired gospel of the Carter Family with the rockabilly sound of her ex-husband, Nick Lowe, Carter has forged a mature style that is uniquely her own.

Most fans find it hard to believe that Carlene has a daughter in college. Tiffany, born when her mom was just 16, helped out as a guitar tech on Carlene's 1991 tour.

Rosanne Cash may belong to one of country music's most famous families, but she came to country music stardom through a side door. She recorded her first album in Germany, her second in Los Angeles. Her hair, over the years, has changed from inky black to eggplant to light brown and back to natural black. She was openly critical of the old Nashville music industry and has never paid attention to the formulas adhered to by nearly all country hit-makers, big and small.

Above: Rosanne Cash posed backstage with her father, Johnny Cash, at Radio City Music Hall after he received a Grammy Living Legend Award. During the tribute to all the winners, Rosanne performed her hit, "Tennessee Flat Top Box," a song written and originally recorded by her father in 1958.

She was also the only woman to have a number-one country album through the early and mid-1980s, reaching the top spot with *Seven Year Ache* in 1981 and *Rhythm and Romance* in 1985. Her first number-one country song, "Seven Year Ache," also reached number 22 on the pop radio charts. Since then, she has topped the country charts 11 times. For her part, the singer says she doesn't try to set trends, she just ignores them.

Cash was born in Memphis on May 24, 1955, just days before her father recorded his first songs at Sun Studios. At age 11, she moved with her father and mother, Vivian Liberto, to Ventura, California. Her father divorced Vivian, his first wife, shortly afterward. Rosanne remained with her mother in California and maintained a close relationship with her absentee father.

After high school, she joined her father's road show, first as a wardrobe assistant and later as a backup singer. She left the band to live in England for a year, then returned to study drama at Vanderbilt University in Nashville and the Lee Strasberg Institute in Los Angeles.

In 1978, she met singer Rodney Crowell, a singer-songwriter who had just released his solo debut album, *Ain't Living Long Like This*. Crowell helped her produce some songs, which led her to travel to Germany to record her first album for Ariola Records.

A CBS Records executive heard the album at her father's house and signed her to a recording contract. With Crowell producing, she recorded *Right or Wrong*, released in 1979. She and Crowell were married early that year

Left: Cash admits to having suffered intense stage fright at one point in her career—so bad, in fact, that she would become rigid prior to performances. She has gained new confidence in recent years, and now enjoys the intimacy of performing. Below: Cash has helped to broaden the definition of country music. "I never bought into the idea that there is a formula," she says. "I still don't."

and had their first child in late 1979. The couple moved to Nashville, where Cash recorded *Seven Year Ache* in 1981. The album established Cash as an effective vocal stylist and revealed her newfound, archly personal songwriting abilities.

Cash records and tours less frequently than most country performers, devoting time to motherhood (she has three daughters), painting, and writing fiction. Her subsequent albums — *Somewhere in the Stars*, *Rhythm and Romance*, *King's Record Shop*, and *Interiors*—have often explored her turbulent relationship with Crowell, addressing the ambiguities of modern relationships with honesty, strength, and intimate insight. The couple separated in 1991.

Mark Chesnutt felt strongly that his first nationally released song, "Too Cold at Home," would become a country radio hit. After all, he had already achieved success with the song three years earlier in Texas. He was right. "Too Cold at Home" helped establish Chesnutt as one of the new traditionalists currently changing the look and sound of country music. Chesnutt was only 26 years old when he was exposed to a national audience for the first time, but he'd already racked up a decade of experience singing in honky tonks and beer joints across Eastern and Central Texas.

Right: Mark Chesnutt achieved an astounding five number-one songs from his debut album. They were "Too Cold at Home," "Brother Jukebox," "Blame It on Texas," "Your Love is a Miracle," and "Broken Promise Land." Chesnutt's devotion to a traditional sort of country sound had paid handsome dividends.

He was born in Beaumont, Texas, a blue-collar town of factories and oil refineries in East Texas. His father, Bob Chesnutt, was a regional country music performer who spent the late 1950s and early 1960s searching for his big break. After one last fruitless trip to Nashville, the elder Chesnutt quit the music business in 1970 to spend more time with his family.

As a young child, Mark absorbed the favorite country music records of his father, whose tastes ran strongly toward George Jones, Merle Haggard, and Hank Williams. By adolescence, he knew he wanted to seriously pursue a musical career. When Mark was 15, his father decided it was time to take him out and introduce him to local nightclub owners. The youngster began performing three or four nights a week while still in high school.

He began recording songs for regional, independent labels in Texas in 1982. "Too Cold at Home," a tune Chesnutt came across while on a trip to Nashville, was the eighth song he had released in Texas. It also became his most successful record.

A regional promotion man for MCA Records in Houston heard the song and sent a tape to Nashville. MCA vice president and chief talent scout Tony Brown quickly arranged to see the singer in Texas. Brown took with him record producer Mark Wright, who had worked on country superstar Clint Black's debut.

Brown signed Chesnutt to MCA. Wright ended up producing the *Too Cold at Home* album as well as cowriting two of its number-one hits, "Blame It on Texas" and "Your Love Is a Miracle." Other successful singles from the album include "Brother Jukebox" and "Broken Promise Land." Wright also produced Chesnutt's follow-up album, *Longnecks and Short Stories*, released in March 1992.

Mark's success has fulfilled his ambition of making a full-time living as a country music singer. His only other job was in the lawn and garden department at Montgomery Ward. His success also brought to reality a dream of his father's. Bob Chesnutt died in November 1990 of a massive heart attack, living just long enough to see his son's first song climb toward the top of the country music charts.

Chesnutt leans heavily on jukeboxes, and for good reason. His second big hit was "Brother Jukebox," a song written by Paul Craft and originally recorded by the late Keith Whitley. Chesnutt also was given a Jukebox Award by the American Music Operators Association as the top new male singer of 1991.

With his handsome, movie-star looks, Billy Dean seems to belong on the big screen as much as he does on the radio. For a while, he did make a living as an actor, appearing in commercials for McDonald's, Chevrolet, and Valvoline Motor Oil. He even had a supporting role in the highly acclaimed but short-lived ABC-TV series *Elvis*. For Dean, acting was just a way to pay the bills. Music has always been his first love.

Above: Billy Dean's handsome good looks contributed to his past success as an actor. Today, he keeps fit on the road with basketball and karate; he has a green belt.

Dean grew up in Quincy, Florida, and began his musical career singing in his father's band. A mechanic by trade, Billy Dean, Sr., taught his son to play guitar and encouraged him to develop his musical talent. Dean touts his late father as a major musical influence, along with more recognizable names such as Merle Haggard, Jim Reeves, Marty Robbins, and Dean Martin.

Dean attended East Central Junior College in Decatur, Mississippi, on a basketball scholarship. After a brief move to Las Vegas, he returned home in 1982, crossed the state line to Georgia, and entered the regional Wrangler Country Star Search talent contest in Bainbridge. After winning the state final, he advanced to the national contest, held at the Grand Ole Opry in Nashville. Although he didn't

win the national prize, he was one of the top ten finalists. More importantly, he decided to extend his visit to Music City into a more permanent venture.

To support himself, he formed a band and started to tour, opening shows for such name acts as Mel Tillis, Gary Morris, Ronnie Milsap, and Steve Wariner. He began to concentrate on songwriting as well, enjoying a fair degree of success when Milsap, Randy Travis, the Oak Ridge Boys, Les Taylor, the Bama Band, and Shelly West recorded his songs. Eventually his songwriting and singing caught the ear of publisher-producer Jimmy Gilmer. Songwriter Verlon Thompson, a friend of Dean's, introduced some of Billy's tunes to Gilmer. Recognizing Dean's abilities, Gilmer quickly signed him to a songwriting contract in 1988. A

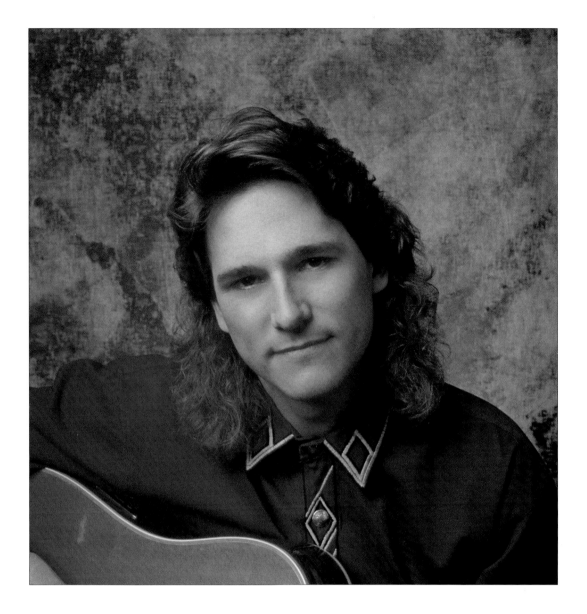

A highlight of Dean's career was being named as one of the ten preliminary finalists for the Country Music Association's Horizon Award in 1991. This recognition made it abundantly clear that Dean had much more going for him than a handsome face.

record deal with Capitol-Nashville/SBK soon followed.

On "Only Here for a Little While," Dean's first single and music video from his debut album, *Young Man*, the handsome performer demonstrated a boyish appeal combined with remarkable talent. The follow-up single, "Somewhere in My Broken Heart," which he cowrote with award-winning songwriter Richard Leigh, showed the more emotional side of Billy Dean to country audiences. The song not only hit the top of the country charts, it also received airplay on adult contemporary radio stations and reached the top ten on the A/C charts. Dean also received a Grammy nomination for best country performance by a male for this smooth, romantic hit. Dean followed this impressive first album with *Billy Dean*, which showcased his sensitive, personal side on such tunes as "Small Favors" and "You Don't Count the Cost."

A talented songwriter, a clear-voiced singer, and a handsome actor, Billy Dean is destined to break a lot of hearts in the years to come.

When "Meet in the Middle" hit the top of the country charts, Diamond Rio stepped into country music history. Never before had a vocal group claimed the number-one position on the national country charts with a debut single.

Six world-class musicians comprise the group Diamond Rio. Each brings a different influence to the band, which accounts for its contemporary, progressive sound. Lead singer Marty Roe seemed destined for a career in country music from childhood. He was named after legendary singer-songwriter Marty Robbins; he learned his first song—Merle Haggard's "The Fugitive"—at age three; and he began his professional career at age 12.

Right: Diamond Rio has enjoyed great sales success, and success of another sort, too: Their song "Mama Don't Forget to Pray for Me" inspired at least one teenage runaway to return home.

While enrolled in David Limpscomb University in Nashville, Roe gained experience by touring with a group called Windsong. In 1984, he joined the Tennessee River Boys, which eventually evolved into Diamond Rio. Lead guitarist Jimmy Olander's talent for music was evident in childhood as well. He was teaching banjo by the time he was 12. Olander performed with such nontraditional country performers as Rodney Crowell, Duane Eddy, and the Dirt Band before hooking up with Diamond Rio. A renowned guitarist, Olander is known for combining technical virtuosity with state-of-the-art instrumentation.

The remaining band members are as talented as they are diverse. Gene Johnson adds mandolin magic to the band's unique sound. Also a top-notch fiddler and acoustic guitar player, Johnson previously played both live and in the studio with J.D. Crowe & New South and David Bromberg. Dan Truman, a classically trained pianist, is a former member of

Brigham Young University's Young Ambassadors. With that group, he toured the world performing for distinguished audiences, including Indian prime minister Indira Gandhi. Bass player and vocalist Dana Williams is the nephew of bluegrass performers Bobby and Sonny Osborne. Williams began playing bluegrass music for a living at the age of 12. Finally, drummer Brian Prout brings a rock influence to Diamond Rio. A native of New York, he moved to Nashville while still a member of a band called Heartbreak Mountain, which also spawned Shenandoah's Marty Raybon. Prout is married to Nancy Given, a drummer for the all-female country band, Wild Rose.

Arista Records' Tim DuBois signed Diamond Rio to a recording contract after seeing them open a show for George Jones. Still known as the Tennessee River Boys at the time, they took the name Diamond Rio from a

type of truck manufactured in Harrisburg, Pennsylvania, because it sounded contemporary. They later visited the Diamond Reo facilities and received a mud flap as a souvenir. They then realized that they had misspelled "Reo," but they kept the erroneous spelling because of its Southwestern flavor.

With "Meet in the Middle" to their credit, Diamond Rio was nominated as vocal group of the year by the Country Music Association in 1991. Their second single, "Mirror, Mirror," climbed to the top half of the charts, eventually settling at the number-three position. Despite being relative newcomers to the charts, Diamond Rio has managed to combine its eclectic influences, ranging from bluegrass to rock to jazz, with a solid country foundation to become one of country music's most riveting bands.

Diamond Rio appeared at their first International Country Music Fan Fair in Nashville in 1991. While there, they enjoyed the opportunity to meet with fans who like their tight, contemporary sound.

Neo-traditionalist Joe Diffie launched a singing career in 1991 that took off instantly and shows no signs of slowing down. His debut single, "Home," was the first record to ever take the number-one position on all three national country charts (*Billboard*, *Radio & Records*, and the *Bill Gavin Report*) in the same week. It was also the first song to hold that position for two consecutive weeks in both *Gavin* and *R&R*. In addition, Diffie became the first artist in the history of Epic Records to hit the top of the charts with a debut single.

Right: One of Joe Diffie's hits, "New Way to Light Up an Old Flame," brought a troubled family back together. A 15-year-old fan told the singer that, after hearing the song, his parents decided against divorce and reunited.

"Home" may have been the first milestone in Diffie's career, but it was quickly followed by three other singles that hit number one—"If the Devil Danced in Empty Pockets," "If You Want Me To," and "New Way to Light Up an Old Flame," all from Diffie's debut album, *A Thousand Winding Roads*. Diffie's freshman year as a country performer represents quite an auspicious beginning.

However, Diffie paid his dues for nine years before savoring this first taste of success. Back in his hometown of Duncan, Oklahoma, he used to spend his days working at a foundry and his nights playing local clubs. When the foundry closed and his marriage failed, he decided it was time to

move to Nashville. "I realized I didn't have anything to lose, so I decided to try breaking in as a songwriter," he recalls. "I'd already had a song cut by Hank Thompson called 'Love on the Rocks.' My mother had sent it to him, and he liked it."

Arriving in Music City in December 1986, Joe found work at the Gibson guitar factory, where he stayed for a little over a year. Fortunately for Diffie, his next-door neighbor was Johnny Neal of the Allman Brothers Band. Neal helped the hopeful singer secure a writing contract with Forest Hills Music. Starting out as a songwriter before launching a career as a performer is standard procedure in country music.

Once established as a staff writer, Diffie began singing on demo records. He quickly became one of the most sought-after demo singers in town.

Diffie hit it big with his debut single, "Home," and his career has continued to roll along in high gear. By cultivating a voice and manner that recall the essence of much of the great country music of the past, Diffie has become an excitingly honest performer.

Almost every music publisher in Nashville wanted to use Diffie's voice to sell their songs. For example, Diffie's was the voice that Ricky Van Shelton heard when "I've Cried My Last Tear for You" was pitched to him.

One of his demo tapes eventually landed Diffie a recording contract. Publisher Johnny Slate had been pitching "New Way to Fly," which was written by Garth Brooks and Ken Williams, with a demo recorded by Diffie. Slate was trying to interest Bob Montgomery of Epic Records in the song. Instead, Montgomery was greatly interested in signing Diffie, even though he didn't have an open slot on his roster. The straight-shooting Diffie promised to wait until Epic was ready for him despite offers by other labels.

Both sides were rewarded a year later when Diffie began making history for Epic Records.

Vince Gill was one of the best-kept secrets in Nashville for many years. The stardom predicted for this highly respected singer-musician always seemed just beyond his grasp. Then in 1990, he released a tune called "When I Call Your Name," and the song went to the top of the charts. Country music audiences finally realized that Vince Gill had arrived!

The only child of an Oklahoma City appellate judge, Gill credits his father, who played banjo and guitar, for piquing his interest in music. One of the first instruments young Vince played was his dad's banjo. An aspiring musician from an early age, Gill joined a local bluegrass band, Mountain Smoke, while still in high school.

Both pages: Vince Gill's haunting tenor voice is an important part of his considerable appeal. Unlike other male country stars, Gill has avoided cowboy hats since being told by a lighting director that people would never be able to see his face beneath the shadow cast by the brim.

Word quickly spread about the budding young musician with the high, lonesome voice. Coincidentally, just as his musical reputation was formulating, Gill—an avid, accomplished golfer—was seriously considering a career in professional golf. The PGA was beckoning when he was invited to join a band called the Bluegrass Alliance, whose membership included bluegrass luminaries Sam Bush and Dan Crary. Loading his possessions into a van, Gill chose to follow his musical instincts and move to bluegrass country—Louisville, Kentucky.

Throughout the late 1970s, Gill paid his dues with a number of diverse bands and musical groups. In 1975, he joined Ricky Skaggs in a band called Boone Creek. The group struggled along with an innovative bluegrass style that featured steel guitar and drums. When Byron Berline invited Gill to join his group, Sundance, on the West Coast, the accomplished picker loaded his van once more and headed to Los Angeles. The job with Sundance turned into a steady gig that lasted over two years; then the boyishly handsome musician changed bands once again. In

Gill is more than a great singer and songwriter—he's also one of the most talented guitar players in Nashville. Vince is well known around town for his "hot licks."

1978, the popular country-rock group Pure Prairie League held auditions for a new lead singer. Gill accompanied a friend to the audition strictly out of curiosity. Mountain Smoke had opened for Pure Prairie League years before, and he wanted to see if they remembered him. Not only did they remember him, they offered him the job as lead singer.

Gill's vocals, guitar playing, and songwriting guided Pure Prairie League to two top-ten hits, "Let Me Love You Tonight" and "Still Right Here in My Heart." Five of Gill's original compositions were included on the group's 1980 album, *Can't Hold Back.*

After Pure Prairie League's record sales began to slump and his wife, Janis (who later founded Sweethearts of the Rodeo with sister Kristine Arnold), became pregnant, Gill left the group to join Rodney Crowell's promising band, the Cherry Bombs. "The level of musicianship in that group was astounding," he once proclaimed to *Country Music* magazine. "I found myself playing with people I'd idolized since I heard them on Emmylou Harris's early albums...Crowell, Larrie Londin, Albert Lee, Emory Gordy, Jr. They all knew exactly what they were doing, and if you didn't stay on your toes, they'd LAP you QUICK!"

Through his friendship with the other Cherry Bombs, Gill landed his first solo record deal. Tony Brown, former keyboard player in the band, worked for RCA Records; and, recognizing Gill's guitar mastery and distinctive voice, Brown signed him to the label. Shortly after moving to Nashville in 1984, Gill recorded his six-song mini-album, *Turn Me Loose.* The success of the title track and "Victim of Life's Circumstances" brought him his first taste of national acclaim as a solo artist. He took home his first award when the Academy of Country Music voted him top new male vocalist.

Gill's second album, *The Things That Matter,* yielded two top-ten hits, "If It Weren't for Him" (a duet with Rosanne Cash) and "Oklahoma Borderline." He gained even more critical acclaim for *The Way Back Home,* his final album for RCA. One tune from that collection, "Everybody's Sweetheart," caught the attention of the Nashville music industry and set gossipy tongues wagging. Rumors circulated that Gill was jealous of his wife's successful career. He did write the tongue-in-cheek song about Janis, but he explained to detractors that it was all in fun. After all, he had helped Sweethearts of the Rodeo secure their record deal by taking their demo tapes to CBS Records.

Despite having a steady string of hits, Gill failed to catch the attention of a broad range of fans, and RCA dropped him from its roster. Fortunately for Gill, Tony Brown, the man responsible for his RCA deal, had moved over to MCA Records. Still convinced that Gill could be a star, Brown signed him to MCA and became his producer.

With a new label and new producer, Gill found the freedom to utilize the full range of his talent on *When I Call Your Name*. The album contained tunes ranging from dance hall swing to contemporary pop to rodeo songs. The first single, "Never Alone," which Gill wrote with Rosanne Cash, hit the top 20. The follow-up, "Oklahoma Swing," was an uptempo, foot-tapping duet with fellow Oklahoman Reba McEntire. The tune, which climbed to the top ten, resulted in a nomination for Gill and McEntire as best duet from the Academy of Country Music.

The popularity of "Oklahoma Swing" laid the groundwork for "When I Call Your Name." With labelmate Patty Loveless providing haunting harmony vocals, Gill enjoyed his first number-one hit with "Name" and won a Grammy Award for best male country vocal performance.

In the fall of 1990, Gill gladly accepted the CMA award for single of the year for "When I Call Your Name,"

starting a chain reaction of awards and some much-deserved recognition. With Loveless, Gill performed this popular tune on the awards telecast and electrified not only his peers, but the national television audience as well. In short order, the MCA album was certified gold and then platinum. It also launched another hit single, "Never Knew Lonely." The following year, "When I Call Your Name" was elected best country song at the Grammy Awards, and Gill added another trophy to his collection.

Having proven his versatility with a wide range of songs on *When I Call Your Name*, Gill settled into a more clearly defined country style for his next album, *Pocket Full of Gold*, which was certified gold just five months after its release. The title tune, "Look at Us," and "Liza Jane" became instant hits. Still reaping awards from his wave of success, Gill was a big winner at the 25th Annual Country Music Association Awards. He shared song of the year honors with Tim DuBois for "When I Call Your Name" and was also named male vocalist of the year. As a member of the talented group who bill themselves as the New Nashville Cats, he shared vocal event honors with longtime friends Mark O'Connor, Ricky Skaggs, and Steve Wariner.

Still a golfer, Gill, wife Janis, and their daughter, Jennifer, live in their dream house next to a golf course in Nashville. Gill once joked that if he didn't make it in music, he could still join the PGA, but he has more than fulfilled his dreams of stardom. He became a member of the Grand Ole Opry in 1991.

One of the most memorable achievements of Gill's career was becoming a member of the Grand Ole Opry. Here, he shares a special moment with the legendary Roy Acuff.

Skilled enough at golf to have once considered turning pro, Gill lives next door to a golf course. Looking for Vince? Check the links!

One of the reasons country music became so popular in the early 1990s was its appeal to a wide range of female fans. A variety of handsome country singers arrived on the scene and were quickly dubbed "country hunks," or "hunks in hats" by the entertainment press. Riding the crest of that wave of popularity was Alan Jackson, who drove the women wild in his concerts and made the men stand up and holler. Some female fans were chagrined to know that Jackson had been happily wed since 1980; others found him all the more appealing because of his devotion to his wife, Denise. In fact, Denise was largely responsible for his musical career.

Above: Alan Jackson and his wife, Denise, make one of the most striking couples in Music City. He wrote "I'd Love You All over Again" to celebrate their tenth anniversary. *Opposite:* Quiet and soft-spoken during interviews, Jackson is a dynamic presence onstage.

In 1985, after a series of jobs that included everything from building houses to driving a forklift at K-Mart to selling shoes to waiting tables at a barbecue restaurant, Jackson decided it was time to make the move from Newnan, Georgia, to Nashville. He wanted to try his hand at a career in music, though he had no idea where to go or who to see.

Denise, who had just quit teaching to become a flight attendant, saw singer Glen Campbell waiting for his luggage at the Atlanta Airport and introduced herself. Explaining that her husband was about to move to Music City to pursue a career, she asked Campbell his advice. He gave her the name of his publishing company in Nashville and told her to have Alan drop by once they got to town. Armed with Campbell's business card, a suitcase full of original songs, and a heart full of dreams, Jackson, with Denise at his side, relocated to Nashville.

He had lined up a job at a boat factory, but when he walked into the metal building filled with fiberglass fumes, he knew he couldn't take the job. Instead, Jackson headed for the personnel office

Even when rehearsing for an appearance on the CMA Awards show, Jackson pulls out all the stops. The Arista Records star is one of the most self-assured performers in country music.

at The Nashville Network and landed a job in the company's mailroom. He became friends with Randy Travis when Travis was working as a singer and short-order cook at the Nashville Palace. Jackson recalls stopping by to congratulate Travis when his first records were taking off, wondering at the time if the same thing would ever happen to him.

Jackson began playing gigs at local hotels during the evenings. He put in countless hours polishing his songwriting skills and eventually landed a writing deal with Campbell's publishing company. With a $100-a-week draw as a staff songwriter, he was able to quit the mailroom job and put his own band together. Booked by Campbell's organization, Jackson and the band played

honky tonks all across the country, five sets a night, five nights a week. Despite the hectic touring schedule and popularity he enjoyed on the club circuit, Jackson failed to stir any interest with the record companies.

His publisher put him in touch with Barry Coburn, an ambitious young manager from Australia. Coburn became Jackson's manager because he recognized the singer's star quality—his all-American good looks, a sincere, traditional vocal style, and songs that had "hit" written all over them.

Timing is everything, and Jackson's timing was impeccable. Arista Records had just opened a country division in Nashville headed by Tim DuBois, former manager and producer of Restless Heart. DuBois was looking for a great talent to launch Arista in Nashville, and he found that talent in Alan Jackson, who signed with the label in September 1989.

One month later, Jackson's debut single, "Blue Blooded Woman," reached radio stations nationwide. The accompanying music video gave female fans their first look at the blond, blue-eyed Jackson. When the record faded after a respectable run, country audiences cried out for more.

Arista responded with the title cut from Jackson's debut album, *Here in the Real World*. On April 6, 1990, the humble Georgia native celebrated his first number-one record. The ensuing singles "Wanted," "Chasin' That Neon Rainbow," and "I'd Love You All over Again" also hit number one, which spurred sales for *Here in the Real World*. The album soared to the number-four spot on *Billboard*'s country album chart and stayed in the top ten for over a year. It was certified gold by the Recording Industry Association of America in September 1990 and gained platinum status just six months later. *Here in the Real World* went platinum in Canada and entered the British country charts at number two.

Regarded as a dynamic performer and a seasoned writer who could handle a variety of themes with sensitivity and flair, Jackson also became known as a sex symbol for an increasingly younger country crowd. Female fans, driven to distraction by his down-home charm and handsome good looks, began throwing lingerie at his feet during performances or rushing onstage to wrap themselves around him.

Aside from the adulation of the fans, he also garnered acclaim from the industry. The Academy of Country Music named him top new male artist in April 1991. Five days later, he shared song of the year honors with Mark Irwin for "Here in the Real World" at the Music City News Country Songwriters' Awards. "Wanted," which Jackson also penned, was another of the 1990 top-ten country hits honored that evening. In addition, *Radio & Records*, a leading music industry trade publication, named Jackson the best new artist of the year.

All eyes and ears were on Jackson's second Arista album, *Don't Rock the Jukebox*, which was released in May 1991. He hit the jackpot once more, as fans responded with wild enthusiasm. *Don't Rock the Jukebox* was certified gold just two months after its release and went platinum three months after that.

Working within the solid country parameters that helped establish him as one of Nashville's new traditionalists, Jackson broadened his scope both emotionally and musically on this second album. He conveyed the uptempo side of romance with "Love's Got a Hold on You," but also included such moving ballads as "Someday" and "From a Distance." More interestingly, Jackson indulged in the country singer's tendency to explore his roots and honor his influences. "Just Playin' Possum" featured an aural cameo by George Jones, who had also made a guest appearance in Jackson's "Don't Rock the Jukebox" video. "Walkin' the Floor Over Me" was both a reference to the country standard by Ernest Tubb as well as a twist on it. Finally, the young singer

In the liner notes of his *Don't Rock the Jukebox* album, Jackson thanked Wrangler for extra-long jeans. No wonder, because the leggy singer takes a 38-inch inseam!

offered a haunting meditation on Hank Williams called "Midnight in Montgomery." The entire collection demonstrated Jackson's depth and maturity.

Jackson admits that singing country music was not something he fantasized about as a kid growing up in Newnan. The youngest of five children, his family's sense of well-being was drawn from traditional values rather than material wealth. Because of the shortage of space in the family home, Jackson slept in a hallway until he was ten years old. At that time, one of his four sisters left home for college, and he finally got a room of his own. "We weren't very well-off financially. I didn't realize until I was older that we might have been considered 'poor'. I have good parents. My father might be the only truly good man I've ever known. If I turn out half as good, I'll be happy."

Jackson's father, Eugene, worked as a mechanic for the Ford Motor Company and fostered his son's life-long interest in motor vehicles. By the time he was ten years old, Jackson was driving the family pickup. He bought his first car at the age of 15, a 1955 Thunderbird that he and his father spent a year rebuilding. It's the only automobile he held onto for any length of time, selling it five years later so he could make a down payment on a house.

Alan started singing as a teenager, performing duets with a friend. They eventually put a band together and played on weekends. He never considered a career in music, because in Newnan—as in many small towns—it was expected that he'd do what everybody else did. He'd go to school, get

Since Alan Jackson has become one of country music's most popular stars, his hometown of Newnan, Georgia, has begun celebrating Alan Jackson Day.

Opposite: Despite a hectic tour schedule, Jackson keeps the romance in his marriage by writing songs for the special occasions he shares with his wife.

married, and have a few children. A music career was simply not in the scenario.

He met Denise when he was 17, and they married four years later. While she taught school, the hard-working Jackson held a variety of unsatisfying jobs but managed to make music his hobby. He was in his 20s when he was overwhelmed by an undeniable urge to pursue a career in music. Jackson was inspired by a friend who learned to fly small planes in the hopes of being a jet pilot. Four or five years later, that friend had succeeded and was flying for a major airline. His friend's success story triggered Alan's aspirations to pursue his goal as well. At that point, Denise ran into Glen Campbell at the airport, and Jackson was on his way.

Since his meteoric rise to country stardom, Jackson has become a member of the Grand Ole Opry, performed for President George Bush in Washington, D.C., participated in the inauguration of Georgia governor Zell Miller, and opened over 100 concerts for Randy Travis. Perhaps his greatest thrill, however, was meeting the legendary George Jones. On the liner notes of his debut album, Jackson had referred to one of Jones's biggest hits, "Who's Gonna Fill Their Shoes," when he wrote, "I don't know whether I can fill 'em, but I'd sure like to try 'em on." Since Jackson has become acquainted with Jones, the two have formed a mutual admiration society. Jackson's pickup truck sports a bumper sticker reading "I Love George Jones." Jones has a matching pickup, same make and model, with a bumper sticker that says, "I Love Alan Jackson."

WYNONNA JUDD

When Wynonna Judd stepped onstage at the American Music Awards in Los Angeles on January 27, 1992, the veteran performer embarked on a new career. Already regarded as a country music superstar because of her identity as one half of the Judds, the dynamic vocalist faced a new challenge when she performed "She Is His Only Need." For the first time in her eight years of singing professionally, Wynonna was onstage alone. Her mother and former singing partner, Naomi, was sitting in the audience.

Above: Wynonna Judd has moved and electrified countless fans with her gutsy, one-of-a-kind voice. *Opposite:* As the Judds, mother Naomi (*left*) and Wynonna have been known to have a spat or two in public. But they both believe they are closer than any other two people in the world. Wynonna now faces the challenge of solo stardom.

The mother-daughter duo has enjoyed a sensationally successful career, one that most entertainers only dream of. With their first single release in 1983, "Had a Dream," the Judds began the second phase of their rags-to-riches story.

The first part of that story began on May 30, 1964, when Wynonna (whose given name was Christina) was born in Ashland, Kentucky. When she was four years old, the family, including Naomi (who was christened Diana) and Wynonna's father, Mike Ciminella, moved to Los Angeles, where Wynonna's younger sister Ashley was born. The Ciminellas' marriage foundered, and the couple divorced. At the end of the school year, Naomi moved her two daughters back to Kentucky.

Living in a remote area without a television, Wynonna picked up a guitar when she was 12 years old in order to escape interminable boredom. As she taught herself to play and sing, Naomi would add harmonies.

With her mother attending nursing school and unable to spend a lot of time at home, teenager Wynonna, still sensitive to the subject of her parents' divorce, developed a rebellious streak. Her behavior of breaking curfews, talking back, bossing her younger sister around, and refusing to keep her room in order created tension between mother and daughter. Once when Wynonna stormed out of the house in anger clad only in a slip, Naomi locked her outdoors for a couple of hours.

Fortunately, peace prevailed more often than anger, and Naomi and

Wynonna and her boyfriend, musician Tony King, have been an item for several years, but have found it difficult to make the time to be together. For now, Wynonna and Tony have postponed their wedding plans.

Wynonna practiced their music. Beckoned by Nashville's reputation as the country music capitol of the world, Naomi moved the girls once more. While working as a nurse, Naomi looked after the daughter of record producer Brent Maher. The two remained friends, and Naomi eventually gave him a homemade tape of one of the duo's singing sessions.

With a vision of their superstar potential, Maher found songs for the pair that showcased the best of their voices and personalities. After several months, he persuaded executives at RCA Records to give the two a rare live audition. An hour later, they had a record deal.

As their first mini-album was finished and a tour schedule set, mother and daughter found their relationship at an all-time low. Wynonna, just out of high school, had moved into the home of a family friend. Whenever she and Naomi were around one another, they somehow managed to provoke each other into a fight. When they starting touring, they realized they *had* to work out their problems.

As their musical career progressed, their relationship began to mend. Their second single, "Mama He's Crazy," skyrocketed up the charts in the summer of 1984 to become their first number-one record. Four months later, "Why Not Me" also soared to the top of the charts. The Judds had definitely arrived!

By the end of the decade, they'd scored 12 more number-one hits, including "Girls Night Out," "Love Is Alive," "Have Mercy," "Rockin' with the Rhythm," "Change of Heart," "Young Love," "Turn It Loose," and "Born to Be Blue." Beginning with *Why Not Me*, every album they have recorded has been certified gold, an amazing accomplishment. Adding to that accomplishment is the fact that the first six of those gold albums have also attained platinum status.

Since launching their phenomenal career, the Judds have received every accolade possible in the music industry, starting with the Country Music Association's Horizon Award in 1984. They walked away with a CMA Award every year from 1984 through 1991.

The Academy of Country Music honored the Judds with seven consecutive top vocal duet awards, and they were named duet of the year at the Music City News Country Awards from 1985 to 1991. Other trophies include four International Country Music Awards, an American Music Award, and three Grammy Awards for best country vocal performance by a duo.

In late 1990, when Naomi Judd announced her impending retirement due to chronic active hepatitis, country audiences knew they would miss Naomi but also feared they would no longer hear Wynonna's bluesy, gutsy vocals. For the next year, the duo toured the United States, selling out concert after concert as Naomi bade a genuine goodbye to her legions of fans. It was the most difficult year the Judds had ever faced.

When the Judds appeared together in concert for the last time in December of 1991, the event became the most successful musical concert in television pay-per-view history. Naomi contributed vocals to at least one song on Wynonna's solo album.

Talent and good looks gallop in the Judd family. Ashley Judd (center), Wynonna's sister, is a successful actress who has appeared frequently in *Star Trek: The Next Generation*, and who is a regular on NBC-TV's *Sisters*.

They performed their final concert, which sold out in a record-setting 17 minutes, in Murfreesboro, Tennessee. Made available to pay-cable systems across the country, the Judds' final concert became the most successful musical event in pay-per-view history.

Country music lovers were relieved to find that Wynonna was going to continue her career. Her solo album on MCA Records, titled simply *Wynonna*, was touted as the most highly awaited record release of 1991. The songs selected for the album were kept secret, and only a few lucky music industry insiders were able to hear an advance copy of Wynonna's powerful solo debut.

When Wynonna hit the stage at the American Music Awards, she took the first steps of what is destined to be one of the most successful solo careers in country music history.

KENTUCKY HEADHUNTERS

When the Kentucky Head-Hunters bounded offstage after winning the Country Music Association's prestigious album of the year award in 1990, the program's cohost walked to the microphone beaming with a broad smile. "Country music will never be the same," quipped superstar Randy Travis.

With their debut album, *Pickin' on Nashville*, the Kentucky HeadHunters kicked open a door of new possibilities for country music. The quintet's initial collection of good-time, rockin' country blues has sold more than a million copies and attracted throngs of young, rowdy concert crowds.

Above: Ricky Lee Phelps thanks the audience at the Grand Ole Opry as the Kentucky HeadHunters accept an award for Best Country Vocal Group. *Opposite:* The HeadHunters are (*front, left to right*) singer Ricky Lee Phelps, guitarist Richard Young; (*back, left to right*) bassist Doug Phelps, drummer Fred Young, and guitarist Greg Martin.

Moreover, the group received the backing of their peers and the country music industry leaders. The group's debut album garnered the group many major awards: They were named 1990 group of the year and producers of the year (as well as winning the award for album of the year) by the Country Music Association; they received a Grammy Award for best country performance by a group; the Academy of Country Music named them best new group of the year; *Billboard* magazine named them best group and best new artist; and the American Music Awards honored them as best new artist.

The huge level of success surprised

everyone, including the close-knit band, which consists of two sets of brothers and a cousin. "People are always asking me how it feels to have a gold album or a platinum album," says singer Ricky Lee Phelps. "I tell them that, shoot, I was thrilled to have a black one. Everything that's happened has so far exceeded our expectations that a day doesn't go by that we don't stop and thank the Lord for what's happened to us."

The singer and his brother, bassist Doug Phelps, grew up in Paragould, a small town in eastern Arkansas. Doug met guitarist Greg Martin when the two performed in country singer

The HeadHunters make merry. Ricky Lee Phelps (*back, right*) is a professional juggler who owns a magic shop in Nashville. While on tour, he constantly practices new tricks.

Ronnie McDowell's band. Martin, in turn, introduced his new friend to his cousins, guitarist Richard Young and drummer Fred Young. The latter three grew up in rural Metcalfe County in southern Kentucky.

Martin and the Youngs spent the 1970s performing Southern boogie and hard rock in a band known as Itchy Brother. The band gained a solid reputation in Kentucky and the mid-South. They were preparing to sign a record deal with Swan Song Records when the company's owners, Led Zeppelin, were stunned by the death of their drummer, John Bonham. Itchy Brother continued, but no other recording contracts

materialized. The band broke up in the early 1980s.

Richard Young became a staff writer for Acuff-Rose, a legendary Nashville music publishing firm. Fred Young joined the band of country singer Sylvia. His eclectic experiences even included an appearance as a musician in the film, *Sweet Dreams*, starring Jessica Lange as Patsy Cline. Along with Doug Phelps, the Youngs and Martin decided to start playing together for fun in an old barn called "the practice house" on land owned by the Young family.

Eventually, Phelps's brother Ricky Lee attended a practice. Within minutes, the group says the room lit up. "Something clearly clicked," Richard Young says. "We knew we had something special together that we liked." Among the first songs the group attempted was Bill Monroe's "Walk Softly on This Heart of Mine," done as a big beat, electric barn burner. The song later became their first country music hit.

The quintet christened themselves the HeadHunters (Kentucky was added later for copyright reasons) and decided to take the music off the farm. A few shows in small clubs in Kentucky and Tennessee proved successful and stimulating, and the group decided to make it official and roll the dice. They raised $4,500 to record a self-produced tape. The tape reached Harold Shedd, head of the country division of Polygram Records, who dropped by to see the band play at a Nashville nightclub. He offered them a contract and indicated he'd like to add two songs to the existing recordings and put the collection out as an album.

But, Shedd cautioned the band that the hard-edge of their music would make success a long shot for them and would require extra effort on their part. When "Walk Softly" was sent to radio, Polygram asked group members to call major stations across the United States and ask them to listen to the song and give an honest opinion. Some program directors called their music "too edgy," while others deemed it too much like rock 'n' roll.

The song didn't receive strong radio support, barely rising beyond number 30 on the radio charts. But country video stations gave the "Walk Softly" video persistent air time, a reaction to massive numbers of requests. The group's debut album sold 300,000 copies within the first three months, even with little radio attention. When the similarly jaunty "Dumas Walker" was sent out as a single, radio stations responded. They had little choice, considering the flood of requests many stations received. The song became the group's first top-ten hit.

Ultimately, the debut album remained among country's top five sellers for more than 40 consecutive weeks. Helping to keep sales chugging along were two more hit singles—a cover of Don Gibson's "Oh, Lonesome Me" and "Rock 'n' Roll Angel"—and a high-profile tour as opening act for Hank Williams, Jr., playing for crowds of 10,000 to 20,000 fans a night.

The group hooked up with Williams again following the release of their second disc, *Electric Barnyard*, which featured a hilarious cover of "The Ballad of Davy Crockett," a remake of Bill Monroe's "Body and Soul," and a trib-

ute to a live radio show in Kentucky they once hosted called *It's Chitlin' Time*. *Electric Barnyard* sold a million copies with little support from radio.

Through it all, the group has maintained its eclectic repertoire and anything goes attitude. Concerts regularly feature such nontraditional country fare as Chuck Berry's "Little Queenie" or

an electric rave-up of Robert Johnson's "Crossroad Blues" reminiscent of the version done by Eric Clapton and Cream. Also, Phelps sometimes performs magic tricks, juggles, and twists balloons into animal shapes during concerts.

Meanwhile, members of this shaggy-haired troupe stay true to themselves. They arrived at the Academy of Country Music Awards on a city bus amid long lines of limousines and Rolls-Royces. "We're pretty much down-to-earth people," confesses Fred Young. "If any of us started to get a big head, I think the rest of us would aggravate him to the point where it would make him stop."

The HeadHunters doing what they do best: performing live. A concert might include songs from sources as diverse as Hank Williams, Sr., Led Zeppelin, and blues legend Robert Johnson.

Hal Ketchum spent nearly 20 years building a reputation as a top-quality carpenter, and he approached a career in music with the deliberate patience of a master craftsman. "You get your material together, get everything squared away, get your words in one pile and your musical ideas in another pile, then put them together with care," he once professed. "Measure twice, cut once."

Ketchum uses the analogy to explain why he first achieved country music success at the mature age of 38. It also helps explain why he entered the arena with a smash: Ketchum's debut hit, "Small Town Saturday Night," was the biggest country radio hit of 1991 according to the respected trade magazine *Radio & Records*.

Before "Small Town Saturday Night," his country music breakthrough, Hal Ketchum had been performing music and writing songs for 20 years. He calls his blend of folk and rock "American music."

Ketchum took his time and made sure his introduction to country music came under the right circumstances. He painstakingly sought out the right producers and the right record company contract, turning down several offers and deals along the way because the situation didn't measure up to his standards. When he finally made his first cut, it was right on target.

Singing about a small town seemed natural to Ketchum. He grew up in Greenwich, New York, a town of 2,500 in the Adirondack Mountains near the Vermont border. A talent for music ran in the Ketchum family. His dad, a foreman in a newspaper plant, was a banjo player and a member of the Buck Owens Fan Club. His grandfather was a concert violinist who also played square dances and led a swing band.

As a teen, Ketchum joined a rhythm-and-blues trio as a drummer. At the same time, he became a carpenter's apprentice, and by the 1980s he was an accomplished woodworker and furniture maker. He moved to Gruene, Texas, in 1981, where he did carpentry work and immersed himself in the region's rich folk country music scene. He quietly studied such songwriters as Lyle Lovett, Townes Van Zandt, and Butch Hancock in Gruene and nearby Austin. Before long, Ketchum was performing his own songs in the same nightspots as those respected performers who had influenced him.

In 1986, he recorded his first album, *Threadbare Alibis*, for a small, independent European record company, Line Records. (The album was later released by Watermelon Records in America.) The folk-influenced literacy of his songs and the understated warmth of his voice attracted attention in Nashville.

Ketchum signed first with Forerunner Music, the music publishing company owned by producers Allen Reynolds (who has worked with Garth Brooks and Kathy Mattea) and Jim Rooney (who has helped Nanci Griffith and John Prine). When Ketchum later hooked up with Curb Records, Reynolds and Rooney collaborated with him as coproducers. The result was the critically acclaimed *Past the Point of Rescue*, which featured "Small Town Saturday Night" and Ketchum's second hit, "I Know Where Love Lives."

Ketchum mixed business with pleasure when he married Terrell Tye, president of Forerunner Music, in September 1991. He has two children by a previous marriage.

Above: Ketchum dedicated his hit album to his father. Although the two had fierce disagreements about politics in the 1960s, they do share distinctive, bushy eyebrows. "The Ketchum trademark," the singer says.

Left: Ketchum married Terrell Tye in September 1991. Tye runs Forerunner Music, and Ketchum met her after he began writing songs for the company.

Patty Loveless has heard about the struggles many aspiring singers endure while trying to break into the Nashville music scene. She can also relate at least two cases of the doors of opportunity quickly flying open for a person with talent and good timing.

The first tale starts in 1972 and concerns 14-year-old Patty Ramey, the daughter of a Kentucky coal miner. She travels to Nashville with her older brother Roger and knocks on the office door of Porter Wagoner. Patty plays songs that she wrote herself for the country star. He enjoys what he hears and introduces the singer to his partner, Dolly Parton, who befriends the youngster.

Both pages: Although Patty Loveless beat the odds by becoming a professional singer while still in her teens, subsequent events slowed her career. Today, her crystal-clear vocals have become her trademark, whether she's singing a heart-tugging ballad like "Don't Toss Us Away" or a raucous, uptempo scorcher like "I'm That Kind of Girl."

Not long afterward, the singer opens a concert in Knoxville, Tennessee, for the Wilburn Brothers. Patty Ramey impresses Doyle Wilburn, who signs her and her brother to his publishing company and takes the two on the road as his opening act. Four years later at age 18, she runs off with the group's drummer, Terry Lovelace, and settles in King's Mountain, North Carolina. She spends a decade performing in hotels and honky tonks.

The second tale begins in 1985. A recently divorced North Carolina nightclub singer decides to return to Nashville, where she had found some success while in her teens. Her brother (and former singing partner) helps her finance a recording session. Her brother, with the five-song tape in hand, marches into the office of MCA talent executive Tony Brown. An irritated Brown agrees to hear half of a song, no more. The brother starts a song, and Brown lets it finish. The executive listens to a second, then a third. Two months later, Brown signs Patty Ramey Lovelace to MCA Records, then suggests she change her name. She becomes Patty Loveless.

Loveless and Clint Black share a musical bond— they both bring a contemporary edge to traditional country music.

Since then, Loveless has navigated a steadily climbing career. In 1991, she was nominated for the third consecutive time for female vocalist of the year by the Country Music Association. And her *Honky Tonk Angel* album crossed the 500,000 mark in sales. Her string of successful tunes stretches back through 1987 and includes such hits as "Jealous Bone," "Hurt Me Bad (In a Real Good Way)," "I'm That Kind of Girl," "On Down the Line," "Timber (I'm Falling in Love)," "Chains," "Don't Toss Us Away," "A Little Bit in Love," and "If My Heart Had Windows."

A cousin of Loretta Lynn, Loveless grew up with a similar background: She was a coal miner's daughter from rural Kentucky. She was born in Pikeville—as was her stylistic counterpart, Dwight Yoakam—and her father worked the mines, dying of a heart attack at age 57. When Loveless was ten years old, her family moved to Louisville to get medical care required by her father.

Loveless loved to sing as a child. Her mother encouraged her to show off her beautiful voice to visitors, but the young girl was too shy to face an audience. Instead, she hid in the kitchen and serenaded the others as they listened on the opposite side of the door. She also wrote songs prolifically, locking herself in the bathroom so she could find some private space in a home filled with six siblings.

Obviously, Loveless developed her powerful pipes early on. Then, ten years of singing rock music in North Carolina bars increased her range and gave her voice a texture acquired from the strain of singing night-after-night over a loud band in a smoky environment. Her voice is supple and unrestrained, and over the course of five albums she has forged a personal style that blends rollicking country rock, traditional honky tonk, and heart-stirring balladry. Her first top-ten hits indicated her direction early on: the first, a cover of George Jones's aching tearjerker, "If My Heart Had Windows"; the second, "A Little Bit in Love," a jaunty, rockabilly-influenced tune written by Steve Earle; the third, a contemporary country rocker, "Blue Side of Town."

Like the little girl who hid behind the kitchen door, Loveless's strong voice is balanced by a shy, almost awkward stage presence that draws an audience toward her. Even after two decades of performing, she still doesn't rely on the kind of confident stage professionalism that can seem insincere and overly slick. Loveless appears comfortable only when she's singing, and she pours herself into her songs with genuine conviction.

Nonetheless, her music takes risks few other country stars dare. From the forceful plea of "Don't Toss Us Away" to the gritty realism of "The Night's Too Long," Loveless has shown a willingness to draw on writers from outside of Nashville and to offer idiosyncratic stories alongside her more immediately accessible work.

Loveless's story is rich with unconventional decisions and unusual twists of fate. For instance, she had lost track of the progress of country music after leaving Nashville for North Carolina. For years, Loveless couldn't sing country music because club owners and audiences didn't want it. But then, she started hearing requests for songs she'd never heard. "Mama He's Crazy," crowds would yell out, but Loveless was unfamiliar with the Judds. "How Blue," yelled others, but the singer hadn't heard of Reba McEntire. To investigate, she bought a few country cassettes and found out Nashville had rediscovered the kind of country music Loveless originally loved.

She telephoned her brother, Roger Ramey, who had remained in Music City USA to work within the music industry.

Above: Loveless has been writing songs since she was a teenager, but her hectic touring schedule over the past few years has prevented her from writing as much as she'd like.

Left: When Loveless is on stage, she is completely at ease, and ignites audiences with her forceful vocals and free-spirited energy.

He confirmed her suspicions and encouraged her to come back and take part in Nashville's new youth movement.

Like Reba McEntire and Kathy Mattea before her, Patty Loveless's climb up the ladder of success was slow, steady, and filled with personal growth and memorable music. Her career highlights include joining the Grand Ole Opry; performing in Farm Aid II; touring with such superstars as Clint Black, Alabama, George Strait, and Hank Williams, Jr.; and winning such awards as favorite female vocalist from the TNN-Music City News Awards, best new country artist from the American Music Awards, and star of tomorrow from Music City News.

LYLE LOVETT

Lyle Lovett likes to toy with conventions. He's a fourth generation Texan, but he's afraid of cows. He wears his hair tall, not short or long. He's touted as a country singer-songwriter, and while he does play shuffles and waltzes, he's just as likely to play honking blues or swinging jazz or somber folk music.

Lovett uses his quirky views on life and love as his calling card. Though he hasn't achieved broad radio airplay, his three albums on MCA have sold well thanks to positive reviews, widespread television exposure, and strong word-of-mouth among fans.

Above: Lyle Lovett admits his hair has grown into something of a gimmick. He cultivated his high-rise hairdo, he says, "because I hated my face. I figured the more people notice my hair, the less they will notice my face." But Lovett's hair isn't really the issue—his talent and versatility are what have earned him his place in country music.

His artistic standing was underlined when his album, *Lyle Lovett and His Large band* earned him a Grammy in 1989 for best country vocal performance by a male. At the awards show, in typical Lovett fashion, he accidentally dropped the statue as he walked across stage. As he grimaced and picked up the pieces, the crowd howled with laughter at his self-deprecating charm.

Lovett grew up in Klein, Texas, on the same plot of land where his great-great grandfather, town namesake Adam Klein, first settled. Today, Lovett lives in a home once owned by his late grandfather, which is part of the ranch where his parents, William and Bernell Lovett, reside and raise cattle.

Lovett began singing and writing songs while earning degrees in journalism and German at Texas A&M. He met singer-songwriter Nanci Griffith by interviewing her for the school paper. With her support, he started playing small nightclubs in Houston, Dallas, and Austin.

While performing in a folk festival in Luxembourg in 1983, Lovett hooked up with the J. David Sloan Band and followed them back to Arizona. Using the Sloan band, Lovett recorded his first songs in a Scottsdale studio.

Lovett took his self-made tape to Nashville, where he received such

encouragement that he returned to Arizona to record 14 more originals. Esteemed songwriter Guy Clark, a newfound Lovett fan, passed the fellow Texan's new music to Tony Brown of MCA Records. Brown added a few instrumental parts to ten of Lovett's previously recorded songs and released them in 1986 as the critically acclaimed *Lyle Lovett*.

The first album revealed a singer-songwriter with a refined, assured vision and a witty way with words. He sang about shaky love affairs, sturdy old porches, and hilarious weddings with sharp insight and a distinctively personal point of view. His first disc also hint-

ed at his ability to write swinging blues vamps with the song "An Acceptable Level of Ecstasy (the Wedding Song)." He expanded upon this talent in *Pontiac* and then fully displayed his ability to blend jazz, blues, and country on his third album, *Lyle Lovett and His Large Band*, which featured his talented, racially mixed, 11-piece touring band on several songs.

By the early 1990s, Lovett had contributed songs to several movie soundtracks. He also contributed a version of "Friend of the Devil" to a collection of Grateful Dead covers called *Deadicated*. His fourth album, *Joshua Judges Ruth*, was released in March 1992.

An imaginative singer-songwriter, Lovett has drawn praise from many of his peers, including Bonnie Raitt, Lou Rawls, producer Don Was, and others.

Kathy Mattea's gradual climb to stardom always carried a hint of the inevitable. She signed her first recording contract with Polygram Records on her 24th birthday on June 21, 1983. Her first hit, "Street Talk," reached its peak of number 25 on the country music charts on the fifth anniversary of Mattea's arrival in Nashville. She enjoyed her first number-one hit, "Goin' Gone," a month after announcing her engagement to songwriter Jon Vezner. Then, exactly a month after their marriage on Valentine's Day in 1988, Mattea's award-winning hit, "Eighteen Wheels and a Dozen Roses," spent two weeks at number one, making her the first female to linger at the top of the country charts for more than seven days since 1979.

Despite the signs that fate was on her side, Mattea spent several frustrating years receiving little recognition. Her initial seven singles from her first two albums failed to crack the top 20. "I knew it would take a lot of hard work, and it did," Mattea recalled. "I worked seven days a week more often than not. But I always felt good about the way things were going. I tried not to let myself get too discouraged."

Her career started to waltz forward in 1986 with her first top-ten hit, the striking "Love at the Five and Dime." The follow-up, "Walk the Way the Wind Blows," also gusted into the top ten as did "You're the Power" and "Train of Memories." This string of successes set the stage for Mattea's jump to consecutive number-one songs and a string of prestigious awards.

The youngest of three children, Mattea was born June 21, 1959, in tiny Cross Lanes, West Virginia, a factory town down river from Charleston. Her father worked at a Monsanto chemical

Mattea wows 'em during a performance during the annual country music Fan Fair, which is held in Nashville each June. Although a serious throat infection caused Mattea to cancel her 1991 Fan Fair performance, she did sit in her booth to sign autographs and communicate with her fans by typing into a computer.

plant, her mother as a housewife. Cross Lanes, she once explained, was named for the one intersection with a stoplight, and the biggest event of her youth occurred when a Burger Chef opened in town.

She attended school in nearby Nitro, and she took piano and tap dancing lessons as a child, moving on to the recorder and the French horn in high-school band class. But her personal musical development began when she learned to play acoustic guitar so she could sing folk songs by Buffy Ste. Marie and Joan Baez while sitting around campfires in her early teens.

In 1976, she enrolled as an engineering student at West Virginia University in Morgantown. She hooked up with a folk group, Pennsboro, trading lead and harmony vocals with other members.

Three years later, the group's lead songwriter, Mickey Pope, announced he was moving to Nashville to chase the big time. Mattea decided to go as well, leaving college despite her parents' objections.

Mattea teamed with Pope as a duo, appearing at songwriter nights until her partner decided to return to West Virginia a year after their arrival. Mattea remained, taking a job at the Country Music Hall of Fame as a tour guide.

She began picking up music jobs as a demo singer, meaning she was hired by writers who needed good versions of their songs on tape to give to producers and record companies. She left the Hall of Fame because the tours forced her to talk all day and put a strain on her voice. Wanting to devote her days to her musical ambitions, she found a compatible night job waiting tables at a busy restaurant near Vanderbilt University. Her natural warmth made her popular with customers, and she attracted attention by tying up her hair and holding it in place by running it through the center hole of a red vinyl record shaped like a heart.

News about this talented, down-to-earth West Virginian spread. She held informal singing parties at her house on 17th Avenue, where friends and guests would pass an acoustic guitar and try out new songs. Soon, she began performing at such popular nightspots as the Bluebird Cafe, where she attracted capacity crowds. That led to her recording contract with Polygram Records.

At first, the singer suffered from a lack of direction. Her debut album touted her as a sensual singer of lushly produced, middle-of-the-road songs. She was dressed in leather pants, skinny ties, and plunging necklines, and most photographs pictured her in aggressively seductive poses.

Producer Allen Reynolds, who has worked with Crystal Gayle, Don Williams, and Garth Brooks, helped Mattea develop her own style as she gained experience. With each successive album, her music grew more sparse and acoustic, her songs more earthy, her image more casual and softly feminine. The husky, fluid warmth of her vocal tone became more prominent, while her arrangements began to showcase the stirring acoustic instrumentation of musicians such as fiddler Mark O'Connor, dobro player Jerry Douglas, banjo player Bela Fleck, and guitarists Pat Flynn and Ray Flacke. Her interest in distinctive songs also surfaced, and her albums introduced many new writers, including Nanci Griffith, Tim O'Brien, Pat Alger, Fred Koller, Alan O'Bryant, Don Henry, and husband Jon Vezner.

Mattea, in interviews in the past, regularly stated that her career demands and nonstop traveling kept her too busy to develop a serious relationship. She dated occasionally, and Vezner, a songwriter from Minnesota, became one of her casual companions. She points to the day when he drove with her to a concert opening for George Strait in Jackson, Tennessee, as the moment when she realized her interest in Vezner had grown deeper. The two talked throughout the five-hour round trip, and she discovered how much they had in common and how much she enjoyed

his company. From there the relationship blossomed.

Mattea was named the female vocalist of the year by the Country Music Association in 1989 and 1990, and she won a Grammy Award in 1991 for her vocal performance on "Where've You Been," a song cowritten by Vezner and Don Henry. The song also won a CMA Award and Grammy Award for the writers. A solid performer, with much experience and talent behind her, Mattea should enjoy a lengthy career in country music.

Mattea remembers people telling her "this is your year" for so long that she had to bite back a laugh every time someone said it. Happily, her year finally did come in 1988 with her album, *Untasted Honey*.

One of the new breed of performers to shake up Nashville in the 1980s, Reba McEntire became the reigning queen of country music by focusing on a traditional sound, recording consistently high quality material, and remaining true to her roots. Along with George Strait and Ricky Skaggs, McEntire helped prove to Nashville that the strength and future of country music lay in its heritage. With over 20 albums to her credit (including nine gold albums, and three platinum), she continues to be one of country music's most popular entertainers.

Both pages: Reba McEntire isn't merely the most successful female vocalist in country music—she's also one of the industry's smartest business people; she maintains her own management, publicity, and music-publishing companies. Blessed with a voice that is as versatile as it is powerful, McEntire seems destined for a long, fruitful career.

McEntire was born in Chockie, Oklahoma, in 1954, the daughter of Jacqueline and Clark McEntire. Because her father was a champion steer roper, Reba, brother Pake, and sisters Susie and Alice grew up traveling the rodeo circuit with their parents. During long stretches of highway, her mother taught the children how to sing harmony. By the time she was in high school, McEntire began to exhibit the influence of both parents. She competed in rodeo competitions as a first-class barrel racer but also sang as part of a vocal group she formed with Pake and Susie. They performed in clubs across Oklahoma for as little as $13 each, sometimes singing from nine in the evening until three in the morning.

McEntire entered Southeastern Oklahoma State University in Durant, Oklahoma, in 1974, where she majored in elementary education. Despite her intentions to finish her education and become a teacher, McEntire was encouraged by her father to pursue a musical career. Singer Red Steagall ("Lone Star Beer and Bob Wills Music"), impressed by Reba's performance of the national anthem at the National Finals Rodeo, helped her land a recording contract.

The feisty redhead debuted on Mercury/Polygram Records in 1977 with the album *Reba McEntire.* One of her early singles, "I Don't Want to Be a One Night Stand," came out about the time she graduated from college. Newly

As her career gained momentum, McEntire felt less constrained by traditional definitions of country music. In search of a novel look for her "Sunday Kind of Love" music video, she donned 1940s-style garb to smashing effect. Both song and video were immediate hits.

married, she and husband Charlie Battles kicked off their honeymoon by visiting radio stations to promote the record.

Slowly, her records entered the charts. "Three Sheets to the Wind," a duet with Jacky Ward (of "A Lover's Question" fame), reached the top 20 in July 1978. Her second album, *Out of a Dream*, spawned the successful singles "Sweet Dreams," "Runaway Heart," and another duet with Ward, "That Makes Two of Us." The determined singer finally hit the top ten in 1980 with "(You Lift Me) Up to Heaven" and "I Can See Forever in Your Eyes," both from her *Feel the Fire* album. The

following year, country fans were hearing more hit songs from the lady with the powerhouse voice, including "I Don't Think Love Ought To Be That Way" and "Today All Over Again." McEntire's modest success soon snowballed, and by January 1983, she had another chart-topping hit, "Can't Even Get the Blues." Producer Jerry Kennedy had planned to give the tune to Jacky Ward, but when McEntire heard it, she insisted that it was her song. Her instincts paid off because it became her first number-one record.

Other female country singers began to follow through the doors she opened, but few had her vocal range. Known for really belting out hard-country tunes, McEntire has remained on top because she can also slide gracefully into a sweet ballad or attach an ache to her voice when singing about heartbreak. In addition to her distinctive style, she became known for addressing a female viewpoint in the content of her songs.

Despite the success she was having with Mercury/PolyGram, McEntire's association with that label ended after the release of the ironically titled "There Ain't No Future in This." McEntire changed to MCA Records where producer Norro Wilson added fuel to McEntire's burning ambition to be a superstar. Her soulful, emotional vocal style emerged in full force with her first album for MCA, *Just a Little Love*. With "Every Second Someone Breaks a Heart," a song that edged closer to rock 'n' roll than she had ever gone before, McEntire showcased her versatility by pushing the boundaries of what constitutes "country." The song represented a calculated move to hold the attention of her younger fans and to build a larger following.

As more and more fans flocked to her concerts, the country music industry recognized her talents and contributions. In 1983, the Country Music Association nominated her for an award as female vocalist of the year as well as for the Horizon Award. Although she didn't take home any trophies that night, she was well on her way to becoming a household name.

A year later, momentum was rolling in her favor as she was named CMA's female vocalist of the year. Indicating the degree to which McEntire influenced the course of country music dur-

ing the 1980s, she won the honor four years in a row, from 1984 through 1987. McEntire is the only female performer in the history of the CMA Awards to hold that distinction.

In 1985, McEntire took more control of her career by coproducing her albums, starting with *Have I Got a Deal for You*. Not only was it a successful career move, but it also indicated her clout in Nashville. Her 1986 album *Whoever's in New England* began a new

Born and raised in Oklahoma, McEntire once devoted much of her energy to rodeo competition. Happily for fans of country music, she forsook barrel racing for vocalizing.

McEntire stepped back in time to shoot the "Cathy's Clown" video. Television star Bruce Boxleitner costarred in the clip, which was filmed on a movie lot in Burbank, California.

phase of accolades and acclaim. In October of that year, she was rewarded with CMA's coveted Entertainer of the Year award. In addition, her recording of "Whoever's in New England" garnered her a Grammy Award for best female country vocal performance.

While she established new standards in country music, McEntire has been unafraid to show the wide range of her talent. Throughout her career, she has demonstrated that she's not intimidated by legendary performances of classic songs. She enjoys the challenge of taking a standard and making it her own, as with "Fancy," formerly a hit for

Bobbie Gentry, and "The Night the Lights Went out in Georgia," a pop hit for TV actress Vicki Lawrence. She's also recorded such familiar standards as Aretha Franklin's "Respect," the old torch song "Sunday Kind of Love," a stunning version of the Everly Brothers hit "Cathy's Clown," and an a cappella rendition of "Sweet Dreams."

McEntire's career flourished, but her marriage to Charlie Battles suffered. In 1987, after 11 years of marriage, she left their 250-acre cattle ranch near Stringtown, Oklahoma, moved to Nashville, and filed for divorce.

In early June 1989, McEntire surprised her fans with an unexpected wedding to manager Narvel Blackstock. Originally a steel-guitar player in McEntire's band, the divorced father of three formed a management company with McEntire shortly after she left her former manager, Bill Carter, in 1987. "Because he was so good at taking charge, I instantly promoted him to bandleader," she explained in *Redbook* magazine. "Then, when my road manager got sick, Narvel took his place. Soon after that, Narvel became my tour manager. Then I moved him up to be my manager. And THIS year, I moved him back down to be my husband!" The two married in Lake Tahoe, Nevada, at a private ceremony attended by only a few family members.

Although she once told a reporter that she never planned to have children, McEntire's newfound happiness with Blackstock changed her mind. She gave birth to their son, Shelby, in February of 1990.

Not content to dominate country music, McEntire has dabbled in acting, beginning with her music videos. She enlisted actor David Keith (*An Officer and a Gentleman; Firestarter*) to appear with her in the video for "What Am I Gonna Do About You," adding a professionalism to the piece beyond the scope of many country videos. She then played a saloon girl opposite Bruce Boxleitner (from the TV series *The Scarecrow and Mrs. King*) in her video for "Cathy's Clown."

Hollywood beckoned soon thereafter, and McEntire appeared in her first feature film. The amateur actress received some good notices for her costarring role, but the film was not what fans might expect McEntire to do. Her film debut was in the science-fiction thriller *Tremors*, which has since become something of a cult classic. Playing opposite Kevin Bacon and Michael Gross, Reba played a survivalist who helped eliminate some giant, man-eating slugs with an arsenal of sophisticated weapons!

Her next role seemed more in keeping with her image. She played opposite Kenny Rogers in a miniseries called *Luck of the Draw: Gambler IV*, which was the fourth project based on Rogers's popular song, "The Gambler." Playing Burgundy Jones, a gun-slinging madam, Reba got a chance to perform with some of TV's classic western stars, including Chuck Connors (Lucas McCain in *The Rifleman*), Jack Kelly (Bart Maverick in *Maverick*), Hugh O'Brian (the title role in *The Life and Legend of Wyatt Earp*), and David Carradine (Cain in *Kung Fu*). The high-profile part in this miniseries helped introduce her to a mainstream audience.

Sadly, her good fortune was matched by terrible tragedy that same year when her road manager and seven members of her band were killed in a plane crash en route to a concert. At the urging of Blackstock, she had skipped the flight, staying behind in San Diego to shake off a case of bronchitis. Always open with her emotions, McEntire shared her grief publicly and found solace and strength in the support of her fans and her peers.

McEntire chose the songs for her next album, *For My Broken Heart*, to help her deal with the sorrow she suffered following the accident. McEntire channeled all of her sorrows into making the album a universal statement on heartbreak and sadness, and her fans responded overwhelmingly. *For My Broken Heart* was certified platinum (signifying sales of more than one million copies) just two months after it was released in October 1991. McEntire reflected, "For me, singing sad songs often has a way of healing a situation. It gets the hurt out in the open—into the light, out of the darkness. I hope this album heals all our broken hearts."

A highlight of McEntire's career was her opportunity to share the stage with George and Barbara Bush during the *25th Annual Country Music Association Awards*. Reba also hosted the show.

Lorrie Morgan performed on the Grand Ole Opry for the first time when she was just 13 years old. The year was 1973, and the Opry was still located at the historic Ryman Auditorium. Following her performance of "Paper Roses," the young singer received a standing ovation—the first at the Ryman in 12 years. Glancing toward the backstage wings, she spotted her mother and father. One look at the tears in their eyes confirmed what she already sensed. She was in the right place—onstage.

Career troubles and great personal tragedy slowed, but did not stop, Lorrie Morgan's well-deserved ascent to stardom. Her early dedication to traditional country music has endeared her to millions of fans.

The urge to be onstage is among Morgan's earliest memories. The youngest child of Anna and George Morgan (a member of the Grand Ole Opry and best known for his hit "Candy Kisses"), Morgan staged "shows" for her family when she was just a child. She would have her sister introduce her, and then using a perfume bottle as a microphone, she would make a grand entrance singing Petula Clark's "Downtown." She even charged admission!

Having the great George Morgan as a father opened a few doors, but there was also a downside. "It was hard to get taken seriously because I was around so much," Morgan reflects. "I was always 'George's little girl.' I guess that's what happens when everybody knows you while you're growing up."

Morgan discovered she had to open some doors on her own. Following her father's death in 1975, she toured with his band and continued to make regular appearances on the Opry. Music became the focal point of her life, and she performed in her share of rough roadhouses and honky tonks.

As she moved forward in her career, the venues she played in began to improve. She spent two seasons with one of the shows at Opryland USA Theme Park. Following her audition, park personnel assigned her to the bluegrass show—a musical genre she had never sung and didn't particularly like. During rehearsals, however, she developed a respect and love for the music that remains today. A two-year stint touring with George Jones proved to be another valuable learning experience. She opened his show with a few songs

and then sang backup for the legendary singer.

Morgan's first recording experience came when she was still a teenager. While working as a songwriter and demo singer for Acuff-Rose Publishing, she landed a deal with Hickory Records and then later with MCA. The latter released a few singles with Morgan in the early 1980s, and she was nominated as best new female artist by the Academy of Country Music in 1984.

Upon returning to Nashville from the awards show, she fulfilled a longtime dream when she became the youngest member of the Grand Ole Opry on June 9, 1984. Though Morgan felt she was surely on the road to success, exec-

Morgan has rebounded from the unexpected death of her husband, singer Keith Whitley, to become one of country music's most emotional performers. Raised in a country-music household, she now gives back the music that inspired her as a child.

utives at MCA wanted her to develop a more refined image. They pressured her to forsake her ties to the Opry because it wasn't sophisticated or "cool." She refused and, on the basis of that refusal, gained an unjustified reputation of being difficult to work with. MCA dropped her from its roster.

Morgan had a daughter to support from an unsuccessful marriage early in her career, so the spirited singer continued to perform in clubs, on demo records, and at the Opry after she was let go by MCA. She first met singer Keith Whitley when he was cutting a demo of "Does Fort Worth Ever Cross Your Mind." At the time, Lorrie thought he was the best-looking man she had ever seen, but because he was married, the two remained only professional acquaintances. When Whitley's marriage broke up, their acquaintance blossomed into romance, and they married in November of 1986. While Whitley's career soared, Morgan's

Morgan and husband Keith Whitley joyously celebrated the birth of their son, Jesse, in 1987. The blonde star also has a daughter, Morgan, from her first marriage.

RCA labelmates Lorrie Morgan and Clint Black have been good friends since touring together in 1991. Morgan met her husband, Brad Thompson, during the tour; Thompson was Clint Black's bus driver at the time.

remained dormant, due in part to the birth of their son in June of 1987.

The following year, still confident she could continue her musical career, Morgan signed with RCA Records. Teaming with producer Barry Beckett, Morgan found a combination of songs that showcased her vocal versatility. "Trainwreck of Emotion," her first RCA single, revealed her melancholy country style and became an instant hit.

She was celebrating the release of her first album, *Leave the Light On*, when tragedy struck on May 9, 1989. Whitley, who battled alcohol dependency much of his adult life, died from alcohol poisoning. Stunned by her husband's unexpected death, Morgan coped the only way she knew how—by going back to work. To everyone's disbelief, she was back on the road within a week of his funeral. Five months to the day after his death, Morgan proudly accepted a Country Music Association Award on Keith Whitley's behalf for best single of the year ("I'm No Stranger to the Rain").

Now with two children depending on her, Morgan resumed a full touring schedule and scored her first top-ten hit, "Dear Me." Three subsequent singles from her debut album—"Out of Your Shoes," "He Talks to Me," and "Five Minutes"—reached the number-one spot on the country charts. Her hard work propelled the sales of her album to gold status in April 1990.

Studio wizardry enabled Morgan to release a duet with her late husband, "'Til a Tear Becomes a Rose." Predictably, the song became an overwhelming favorite among many country fans, resulting in a Country Music Association nomination for vocal event of the year. Morgan was also nominated for the Horizon Award and as female vocalist of the year. When she and Keith Whitley were named the vocal event winners, a teary-eyed Morgan accepted the award.

The next year became the start of a new era for Morgan. She released her second album, *Something in Red*, which featured a more diverse selection of songs in contrast to her melancholy debut disc, *Leave the Light On*. Spurred by hit singles such as the title cut, "We Both Walk," and "A Picture of Me Without You," the album was certified gold by the end of the year. Morgan also remarried in 1991. While touring with country superstar Clint Black in 1990, Lorrie met Brad Thompson, the driver of Black's bus. The two began dating in March of 1991, announced their engagement in June, and were married on October 27 in Madison, Tennessee.

Keith Whitley, 1956-1989

A native of Sandy Hook, Kentucky, Keith Whitley began his professional career while still a teenager, playing in the band of famed bluegrass entertainer Ralph Stanley. Something of a musical prodigy, Whitley teamed with fellow bandmember Ricky Skaggs and released a highly acclaimed bluegrass album, *Cry from the Cross*, in 1971. In the mid-1980s, he landed a recording contract with RCA Records and found success with "Miami, My Amy," "Ten Feet Away," "Hard Livin'," and "Homecoming '63."

Whitley completed another album in 1987, but, unsatisfied with the results, he convinced RCA to shelve the project and let him start over. Acting as coproducer, he went back into the studio and recorded a project he believed in—*Don't Close Your Eyes*. The title cut was released as a single and quickly became Whitley's first number-one record. "When You Say Nothing at All" and "I'm No Stranger to the Rain" also topped the charts.

On May 9, 1989, Whitley was found dead in the home he shared with wife Lorrie Morgan. Overcome by the pressures of success, he succumbed to the alcohol dependency that had plagued most of his adult life. In August 1989, the album Whitley finished one month before his death, *I Wonder What You Think of Me*, was released posthumously. Critically and popularly acclaimed, the album was certified gold the following July.

In 1991, RCA retrieved the project Whitley had shelved and recorded new musical tracks to his vocals. *Kentucky Bluebird* made it clear that his untimely death had left his legacy to country music unfulfilled.

K.T. OSLIN

K.T. Oslin's rise to the top of the country charts was unusual because it came at a time in life when many singers begin to fade from view. For Oslin, who was in her mid-40s when she found success as a country entertainer, it represented the beginning of a new career.

Oslin has experienced a varied life in show business, which has exposed her to different challenges and diverse types of music. Her life experiences resulted in a type of country music that is more pop-oriented and urbane than the heartbreak songs usually associated with female country singers.

Both pages: Mature and sophisticated, singer-songwriter K. T. Oslin is one of the most outspoken performers in country music. Although romantically linked at one time with record producer Steve Buckingham, Oslin has never been married, preferring to live independently.

Born in Crossitt, Arkansas, Kay Toinette Oslin grew up in Mobile, Alabama, and Houston, Texas. As a teen, she discovered rock 'n' roll and the Texas folk music scene. One of her earliest professional experiences was singing in a folk trio with acclaimed country songwriter Guy Clark.

With aspirations toward becoming an actress, Oslin found an outlet for her acting desires in the musical theater, landing a job in the national touring company of *Hello, Dolly!* with Carol Channing. After a year on the road, she was invited to join the chorus of the Broadway company of the show, which starred Betty Grable. Surviving on a chorus girl's pay, she also appeared in *West Side Story*, *Promises, Promises*, and

other Broadway musicals before turning to a more lucrative career singing jingles in commercials. Oslin realized, however, that hawking hemorrhoid preparations and cat food did not satisfy her need to perform.

She developed an interest in songwriting while touring the southeastern United States. "I had read a line on a bathroom wall about '72 or '73," she recalled. "I was doing some college concerts, and we stopped for breakfast in Due West, South Carolina. I had gone to the ladies room and was reading graffiti. I like to read that stuff—usually it's pretty raunchy and mindless and stupid. I'm sitting there reading this sentence that said, 'I ain't never gonna love nobody but Cornell

Crawford.' It literally made me throw back my head and laugh."

With that line emblazoned in her memory, she wrote the song "Cornell Crawford" with a friend who was in the jingle business. By 1981, her songwriting attracted the attention of Elektra Records. But Oslin's first single release, "Clean Your Own Tables," quickly faded into obscurity. The second, "Younger Man," didn't fare much better. Radio programmers thought it was too feminist and might offend their male listeners. Although Elektra dropped her from the label, the assertive Oslin wasn't ready to give up.

Other singers began cutting her tunes, giving Oslin the impetus to continue. Gail Davies had some chart success with "Round the Clock Lovin'," and she selected "Where Is a Woman to Go" (also recorded by Dottie West) as the title cut for her 1985 album.

Oslin persevered, borrowing $7,000 from her Aunt Reba, a stockbroker, to stage her own showcase in Nashville. In the audience the night of her big performance was Harold Shedd, who was producing albums for Alabama at the time. Shedd was impressed with what he heard—a strong woman singing country songs with universal appeal. He recorded three tunes with Oslin in the studio and played them for Joe Galante, then head of RCA's Nashville office. Galante, struck by the quality of the lyrics and the conviction in Oslin's voice, called her the next morning and

Oslin has loved show business all of her life but has learned that there is no guarantee of riches. During her days as a jingle singer, for instance, she earned a modest $38 for her work on a Coca-Cola commercial.

offered her a record deal. Three months later, her debut single for the label, "Wall of Tears," hit the charts where it had a respectable run, peaking at number 40.

With her second single, "80's Ladies," Oslin began to secure a niche in country music by offering contemporary tunes and a cosmopolitan image. By the time she bought a house in Nashville in June of 1987, the "80's Ladies" video had reached number one on Country Music Television. Two months later, the *80's Ladies* album debuted at number 15 on the *Billboard* country album charts. That December, Oslin scored her first number-one record with "Do Ya." The following February, the country-politan singer-songwriter won the music industry's highest accolade, the Grammy, for best female country vocal performance. In April, she was named top new female vocalist by the Academy of Country Music. "80's Ladies" was also named best video. Oslin added a gold record to her credit when *80's Ladies* was certified by the Recording Industry Association of America. She became the first female country artist to have a debut gold album since Anne Murray's *Snowbird* in 1973.

Between awards and accolades, Oslin—called "the Diva" by some Nashville industry people—found time to record "Face to Face," a duet with Alabama's Randy Owen that also hit the top of the charts. By October of

1988, Oslin was riding the crest of her initial wave of success when she was named female vocalist of the year by the Country Music Association. She also became the first female songwriter to win CMA's song of the year award, for "80's Ladies."

To make the most of the publicity and media attention lavished on Oslin because of her success, RCA had released her second album, *This Woman*, in August of 1988. This highly successful follow-up garnered the singer two more Grammys, including one for her performance of "Hold Me," the chart-topping hit from the album. "Hold Me," which she also wrote, won a Grammy as best country song. Other awards followed that year, including being named top female vocalist by both the Academy of Country Music and the Country Music Association. By the end of 1989, both *80's Ladies* and *This Woman* had gone platinum. A sold-out concert that fall—where a handsome newcomer named Clint Black opened for her—seemed like icing on the cake.

Oslin took a much-needed two-year break from touring to concentrate on writing songs for her next album. Fans knew it was worth the wait when Oslin's third album, *Love in a Small Town*, was released in November 1990. More stripped down than her other albums, *Love in a Small Town* showcased her songwriting talents by focusing on earthy slice-of-life vignettes and stories about common folk. The first single, "Come Next Monday," became an instant hit and was accompanied by a video in which Oslin was almost unrecognizable as the Bride of Frankenstein. Always daring to be dif-

ferent and willing to capitalize on her theatrical background, Oslin enlisted actor Ray Sharkey for her "Mary & Willie" video, in which the two portrayed singles who are searching for a dream mate. The ground-breaking video drew both critical and popular acclaim for its innovative concept—Oslin was not shown singing in the clip.

Television executives have also taken advantage of Oslin's acting experience. She guest-starred on the western series *Paradise*, and she was slated to star in a series pilot called *Rachel Gunn, R.N.* She withdrew from that project because she found her character "too mean."

With her sophisticated wit and maturity, Oslin has brought a much-needed female perspective to country music. She once admitted that, as a child, she disliked country music because of its predominantly male point of view. "I hated country music as a kid," she said. "Old men, singing about drinking and cheating on wives didn't compute to a 13-year-old. 'Take me back, you're the woman and I'm the man.' If he cheated on me, I wouldn't take him back!"

Oslin's performance on the 1988 Country Music Association Awards show brought a sophisticated glamour to the event. She continues to be a trendsetter via her music and clever, often surprising videos.

COLLIN RAYE

Collin Raye understands the importance of endurance. As a boxing fan and an accomplished weight lifter, he knows strength comes from hard work, persistence, and stamina. As a singer, he realizes the benefits of these same traits.

A performer since childhood, Raye spent most of the 1980s gaining experience and surviving disappointments. He's seen big breaks turn into empty promises, but he never stopped moving toward his goal and working to improve his talents. His perseverance paid off in 1991 with the success of his debut solo album, *All I Can Be*.

Only 30 years old, Collin Raye has been entertaining crowds for more than half his life. Prior to his first number-one single, "Love, Me," he had been a regional attraction in Arkansas, Texas, Oregon, Washington, and Nevada.

Born Floyd Wray in DeQueen, Arkansas, and known as "Bubba" for most of his life, Raye first appeared onstage at age seven with his family. His mother, Lois, was a regional star in Arkansas, where she once opened a performance at a county fair for Elvis Presley and Johnny Cash. With his father, Floyd, on bass and his brother, Scott, on guitar, his mother performed in the Southeast through the 1960s and 1970s.

In 1980, the two brothers followed their mother to Oregon, and before long the two led a popular country-rock band that worked throughout the Northwest. Their reputation spread as far as Reno, Nevada, where they became a favorite act in some hotels and casinos.

In the mid-1980s, they received a recording contract from Mercury Records, releasing several singles as the Wray Brothers. Each song resulted in increased attention from radio, but an executive shake-up at the company left the band without a contract. They returned to Reno, where brother Scotty departed to join another group.

Raye started appearing alone, and once again his talents drew praise from critics and adoration from audience members. Producer Jerry Fuller, who had worked with such diverse performers as Moe Bandy, Johnny Mathis, and Ricky Nelson, learned of Raye's talents and offered to work with him. That led to a record deal with Epic. Fuller and Nashville producer Johnny Hobbs coproduced Raye's debut album, *All I Can Be*. The title song became the album's initial hit and included harmony support from Vince Gill. The sec-

ond single, "Love, Me," spent three weeks at number one in early 1992, establishing Raye as a fast-rising country star.

"I think all the work I've done is an advantage for me," Collin says. "A lot of new artists come to their first albums from working other day jobs, and they have to learn to entertain people as they go along. But this is all I've ever done. I've learned how to communicate with audiences and how to get a song across."

"I've always been able to sing with authority," Raye says. "But I think I'm better now because I'm smarter about my voice. Over the years I've learned it's the subtle things that can make a song come across."

MIKE REID

In looking at the awards Mike Reid has accumulated in his 44 years, it is readily apparent that he is not a typical country singer. A case in point: One of the first awards Reid won was the Outland Trophy, which is given to the top college football interior lineman in the nation. Reid's successful college football career at Penn State, where he majored in music, led to the NFL. A first-round draft pick of the Cincinnati Bengals, he was named the AFC Defensive Rookie of the Year in 1970. An All-Pro in 1972 and 1973, Reid announced his retirement from pro football at the age of 28 and traded the pigskin for the piano.

Above: When he was a professional football player in Cincinnati, Mike Reid entertained elementary school children with private concerts. He often had to get their attention by playing the McDonald's theme in the styles of Mozart, Strauss, and Beethoven!

He toured with a couple of bands before striking out as a solo artist, and he openly concedes that his sports background gave his musical career a boost. "In those early years, I was never billed as a singer-songwriter. I was billed always as a former NFL All-Pro. I know people would come in to see me from curiosity—sort of like going to a zoo."

While touring, Reid also concentrated on songwriting. In 1980, he moved to Nashville after a music publisher offered him a contract. Two years later, Reid found himself on the "Inside" track when Ronnie Milsap took that song to number one. Reid became firmly established as a hit songwriter, most notably for "Stranger in My House," which garnered him a Grammy Award for best country song in 1984. His tune "Lost in the Fifties Tonight" received both Grammy and Country Music Association nominations for song of the year. Prominent artists who have recorded his tunes include Kenny Rogers, Tanya Tucker, Anne Murray, Lee Greenwood, Barbara Mandrell, Joe Cocker, the Judds, Alabama, and Bonnie Raitt.

Reid made his recording debut with "Old Folks," a duet with Ronnie Milsap in 1987. Two years later, Steve Buckingham of Columbia Records approached Reid about a recording contract. The result was his debut album, *Turning for Home*, which spawned Reid's first number-one record as a performer, "Walk on Faith."

Although he has made a successful transition from football to music, Reid is still remembered as a hero of the gridiron. In 1987, he was inducted into the National Football Foundation's College Football Hall of Fame.

Above: Reid's songwriting gifts are impressive. Ronnie Raitt has recorded "I Can't Make You Love Me," written by Mike with his frequent collaborator, Allen Shamblin.
Right: Reid performed a medley of his hits on *The 25th Annual CMA Awards* show in 1991.

Ricky Skaggs served an impressive apprenticeship before getting the opportunity to record his own music for a major record company. He quickly proved he'd learned his lessons well, creating 16 top-ten hits between 1980 and 1986 with a fresh sound that updated bluegrass and honky tonk music with breathtaking musical arrangements and a modern rhythmic bounce. The former bluegrass prodigy's success headed country music in a new direction and set the stage for the later stars and the return to traditional sounds.

Ricky Skaggs is a proficient multi-instrumentalist who has won awards for his musicianship as well as for his vocal work. Onstage, he regularly trades off between a fiddle, a mandolin, an acoustic guitar, and an electric guitar. Perhaps his most unusual instrument is his specially designed mandocaster (*far right*), which combines a mandolin with the shape and amplification of an electric guitar.

Skaggs was born July 18, 1954, in Cordell, Kentucky. By age five, his father was giving him mandolin lessons and his mother was teaching him traditional mountain songs. At age seven, the youngster performed on a TV show hosted by bluegrass stars Flatt & Scruggs. At age 15, he joined the band headed by one of his idols, Ralph Stanley. In 1972, at age 17, he recorded an album with childhood friend Keith Whitley, also a member of Stanley's band.

He spent the mid-1970s as a member of several highly acclaimed, progressive bluegrass bands, including the Country Gentlemen, the New South, and his own Boone Creek. Emmylou Harris recruited him to join her Hot Band in the late 1970s, and Skaggs began recording solo albums for an independent label, Sugar Hill Records.

Skaggs's independent recordings paved the way for his first Nashville album for Epic Records. *Waitin' for the Sun to Shine* surprised every country music executive with its huge sales, and it earned Skaggs his first Country Music Association honors. The young singer was named male vocalist of the year and also won the Horizon Award for most significant career growth. His next three albums sold in equally impressive numbers. In 1985 Skaggs was given country music's most prestigious honor: He was named Entertainer of the Year by the Country Music Association. He went on to win Grammy Awards for best country instrumental performance in 1983, 1984, and 1986, and he shared the 1987 vocal duo of the year award with his wife, Sharon White, of the country music band known as the Whites. He also produced Dolly Parton's country music comeback album, *White Limozeen*.

Of his role in revitalizing country music in the 1980s Skaggs says: "I set out to create a more traditional, back-to-basics kind of sound. [I wanted to] bring forth the mandolin, fiddle, banjo, and steel guitars that had really been lost by the wayside. It was something I felt like the fans wanted, and it was certainly something I wanted."

Skaggs is among the few major artists in Nashville who is self-managed. From his office in a high-rise on Nashville's Music Row, Skaggs maintains a music publishing office and a concert booking company, and he oversees all aspects of his career, from approving photographs to signing employee paychecks.

Doug Stone's musical memories go back as far as he can remember. A family snapshot captures three-year-old Doug sitting entranced in front of a record player. At age seven, his mother took him to a Loretta Lynn concert, and the youngster ended up making his stage debut that night at Lynn's invitation.

At age 16, the Georgia native quit school, bought a mobile home with the money he'd earned performing, and built a portable studio of his own. Thus began a journey that included more than a decade of performing in hotel lounges and late-night honky tonks in the Atlanta area.

Right: Promotional material for Doug Stone's first single, "I'd Be Better Off (In a Pine Box)," included the picture of a dinosaur and an announcement that country music was now entering "the Stone Age."

By the mid-1980s, he had tired of the nightly grind and returned to Newnan, Georgia, where his father owned a repair shop for diesel trucks.

Stone—whose real name is Doug Brooks—went to work as a diesel mechanic. He limited his music performances to weekends at the local VFW lodge, where an aspiring manager named Phyllis Bennett spotted him one night. She suggested that she might be able to help him audition for a Nashville producer. Bennett then introduced the singer to Doug Johnson, an up-and-coming record producer who agreed to record three songs Stone had written. When former Epic Records executive Bob Montgomery heard Stone's work, he quickly offered the smooth-voiced Georgia singer an extended recording contract.

Because Garth Brooks had just released his debut album, Epic executives convinced their new singer to change his name. At the time, Doug was writing a song titled "Heart of Stone," and it provided him with his stage name. In the spring of 1990, Epic introduced Stone with the mournful ballad "I'd Be Better Off (In a Pine Box)," the first of several top five country hits for the newcomer in 1990 and 1991. Others included "Fourteen Minutes Old," "These Lips Don't Know How to Say Goodbye," "In a Different Light," and "A Jukebox with a Country Song." His first album, *Doug Stone*, has sold more than 500,000 copies, and his debut hit, "I'd Be Better Off," earned him a Grammy Award nomination in 1991.

Despite the melancholy nature of many of Stone's best-known songs, the Georgian is a personable, witty ball of energy offstage. He talks with a Southern drawl as thick as the red clay of his home state, and he'll openly admit he's survived some mistakes over the years. Born June 19, 1956, the singer has four children, two of whom reside on a ranch in Newnan, Georgia, with Stone and his third wife, Keri. His parents, Jack Brooks and Gail Menscer, divorced when Doug was 12.

"I've had a lot of experience in life, and I think that helps my songs," Stone contends. "If you can draw on your experiences, then you get closer to the truth. That's what country music is about: the truth."

By the time Stone recorded his second album, *I Thought It Was You*, Sony Records had decided to promote him as a ballad singer with sex appeal. The campaign focused on the slogan, "Doug Stone: The Romance Continues."

When George Strait first visited Nashville, he was told his music was behind the times. Looking back, it's clear he was a sign of the times, a bellwether who pointed the way to greater popularity and prosperity for country music.

In the beginning of the 1980s, the prevailing attitude among those running the country music industry was that Strait's blend of western swing, traditional honky tonk, and romantic ballads was old-fashioned and out of style. He was told to throw away his cowboy hat, kick off his boots and slip into leather loafers, and put some flare into his denim jeans or, better yet, change into dress slacks.

Above: The polished brass rodeo-style belt buckle worn by George Strait isn't merely a nod to cowboy fashion. The Texan grew up on a ranch, and owns one today in South Texas. *Opposite:* More than 17 years after Strait joined the Ace in the Hole band, several original members of the group continue to play backup for him.

He was also told to ditch the fiddles and steel guitars and bathe his mellow, deep-toned voice in the more contemporary sounds of strings and synthesizers.

By the end of the 1980s, however, Nashville was singing a different tune, and Strait now stands tallest among the handful of artists who changed the sound and the look of country music. Strait's old-fashioned ways led country to new heights of success and convinced Nashville music executives to give other young, traditional-sounding country artists an opportunity. That trend has provided country music with its biggest

sales boom in history. "I think there was always an audience out there craving traditional country music," Strait contends. "They just weren't getting it until recently. Then a few of us came along who were doing music with this kind of flavor, and country music has gotten bigger and better. If I had a small part in helping that happen, then, hell, I'm proud of it."

In the decade following the release of *Strait Country*, the Texan's 1981 debut album, he racked up 25 number-one songs, five platinum albums for sales of more than one million, and 11 gold

albums for sales of more than a half-million. His concert sales have topped $10 million annually since the late 1980s. He broke Elvis Presley's record for consecutive sold-out shows at the Las Vegas Hilton, and he sold 95,000 tickets in one day for two sold-out performances at the Houston Astrodome. Twice he has received country music's most prestigious annual honor, the Country Music Association's Entertainer of the Year award. And he has been cited as a primary influence by nearly every successful Nashville newcomer. Garth Brooks, for example, once declared that hearing *Strait*

At the 1986 Country Music Association Awards, Strait accepted his second consecutive Male Vocalist of the Year award from Linda Ronstadt, Emmylou Harris, and Dolly Parton.

Country during his senior year in high school convinced him to pay more attention to country music and less to pop and rock.

Through it all, Strait's boots stayed planted to the ground and his head never outgrew his Resistol hat. He's still a soft-spoken, down-to-earth family man who is uncomfortable with off-stage attention and who remains dedicated to performing the same style of music that brought him to the dance.

Strait was born May 18, 1952, the second of three children. His father was a junior-high math teacher and part-time rancher in Pearsall, Texas, a tiny settlement in the South Texas brush country located about 60 miles south of San Antonio. In his youth, Strait learned to ride horses and rope steers. His initial musical experience was singing "Louie, Louie" and other rudimentary rock songs with a garage band made up of high-school buddies. Shortly after graduation, he eloped to Mexico with his high-school sweetheart. Now, more than 20 years later, he and wife Norma still reside in South Texas with their son, George Jr., who was born in 1981.

Strait enrolled in the army in 1971 to help with finances. A year later, while serving as a clerk at the Schofield Barracks in Hawaii, he taught himself to play guitar by studying a Hank Williams songbook. Before long, the base commander recruited the young Texan to lead a country band. The singer's duties during his last year in the service consisted of performing country music on military bases.

Upon returning home, he enrolled in Southwest Texas State University in San Marcos. On campus, he pinned a note to a bulletin board advertising himself as a singer in search of a country band. He got a call from a group calling themselves Ace in the Hole. With Strait as lead singer, the band began performing nightly in honky tonks within a 200-mile radius of San Marcos.

In 1979, Strait received a bachelor's degree in agriculture and started managing the family ranch, which had grown to include more than 1,000 head of cattle by that time. He worked from sun up to sundown on the ranch, which is located in the township of Big Wells,

a brutally hot part of Texas. After a full day's work, he quickly cleaned up and headed out to sing with Ace in the Hole.

The band's popularity grew, and Strait's voice became more confident and flexible with his nightly performances of traditional Texas dance hall music, which included healthy doses of songs made famous by Bob Wills, Hank Thompson, Johnny Bush, Lefty Frizzell, Merle Haggard, and George

The publicity-shy Strait allows few candid shots to be taken of him offstage and grants press interviews only rarely. "I feel real funny talking about myself," he admits.

Jones. Years later, Strait acknowledged that his vocal phrasing carried a debt to Haggard and Jones. He claimed he developed his style by singing their hits night after night and trying to mimic the way they brought out the emotion of the lyrics.

In the late 1970s, Strait recorded a few songs for D Records, a Houston-based company owned by Pappy Dailey, who had given George Jones his first break more than two decades earli-er. Strait's first single, "Ace in the Hole," received enough attention to give him the courage to travel to Nashville. He made the trek three times without getting a response.

In 1979, Strait figured he had given his dream a shot, and it was time to be more practical. He applied for several jobs, accepting a position with a firm in Uvalde, Texas, designing cattle facilities. When he told his wife, she persuaded him to give music one more year.

Since Strait embraced traditional country attire in 1981, many other singers—some of whom have never mounted a horse—have followed suit.

Among his other supporters was Erv Woolsey, a former music industry executive who managed a San Marcos nightclub, the Prairie Rose, where the Ace in the Hole band often performed. When Woolsey returned to the music business as a promotion executive for MCA Records, he stayed in touch with Strait. In late 1979, he helped Strait arrange a Nashville recording session with producer Blake Mevis. The songs recorded during that session earned Strait a recording contract with MCA Records less than six months after he had turned down the job in Uvalde.

The first hit from Strait's debut album, *Strait Country*, was a stripped-down, dynamic Texas two-step titled "Unwound." It became the singer's first top-ten hit, confounding those who thought radio wouldn't accept such a raw, traditional country style. Even champions of the back-to-basics sound were skeptical about his future. John Morthland, a respected country music critic, described *Strait Country* in a 1984 book entitled *Best of Country Music* as "the best shot of straight-ahead Texas honky-tonk since Moe Bandy came along, though...I have to wonder how long he'll last."

More than a decade later, Strait shows more endurance than any other performer whose initial success occurred in the early 1980s. Only Alabama has scored as many number-one country hits since 1981 as Strait.

He has set several standards. In 1987, the Texan's *Ocean Front Property* disc became the first album in country music history to debut at number one on *Billboard*'s country album chart. In 1990, Strait's hit, "Love Without End,

Strait makes no bones about his performance style—he simply concentrates on putting across a song without fanciness or frills. "I don't do a lot of talking onstage," he says. "I don't tell jokes. I don't moonwalk or break dance or do the alligator."

Amen," became the first song since 1977 to remain in the number-one position on the country charts for five consecutive weeks. His "Famous Last Words of a Fool" was the next song to repeat that feat, staying at number one for five weeks in early 1991.

Amid the success, he's also faced tragedy. His daughter Jennifer was killed at age 13 in an auto accident in 1986. At that point, Strait withdrew from interviews for more than a year, and now, he only reluctantly agrees to appear on television or talk to the press. He's extremely private about his personal life and has never allowed cameras into his home in San Antonio or onto his huge ranch, where he raises horses and cattle. For recreation, he likes to hunt and fish, and he's an accomplished horseman and steer roper. Each summer, he and his brother Buddy host a team-roping contest in Texas.

Strait is a man of constants. Erv Woolsey has been his manager from the outset. His road manager was an original member of the Ace of the Hole band, and two other members remain with him today. About the only band changes he's made have involved adding new players. He has coproduced his albums with Jimmy Bowen since 1984. He has maintained the same booking agent, same publicist, and same fan club president over the years.

As for his music, he says: "I can't really see it changing very much. It's not that I set out to create a certain style or to change country music. It's just that I record the songs I like, and I do them in a way that feels right to me. It's worked pretty well so far, so I guess I'll keep doing it that way."

Marty Stuart likes to say he earned his high-school diploma as a mandolin player in Lester Flatt's band in the 1970s and his university degree as lead guitarist in Johnny Cash's band in the early 1980s.

Stuart grew up Philadelphia, Mississippi, where his father was a factory supervisor and his mother a bank teller. He was hired at age 12 to play mandolin with a gospel-bluegrass band, the Sullivan Family. A year later, he was recruited by the late, legendary Lester Flatt after the singer had split from longtime partner Earl Scruggs. After Flatt's death in 1979, Stuart hooked up with another legend, Johnny Cash, performing with him until 1985.

All along, Stuart knew he wanted to create his own music when the time was right. He released two independent albums, *Marty: With a Little Help from His Friends* in 1978 and the acclaimed *Busy Bee Cafe* in 1982 on Sugar Hill Records. Four years later, he joined CBS Records and put out *Marty Stuart*, which featured the top 20 country hit, "Arlene." But CBS and Stuart disagreed on musical direction, so the young veteran went looking for other opportunities.

In 1989, he emerged on MCA Records with *Hillbilly Rock*, an album that took a fresh perspective on indigenous American music by delving back into the place where the roots of country and rock 'n' roll intertwine. "This is not a rockabilly album," Stuart said when *Hillbilly Rock* was released. "This is hillbilly music—with a thwump."

The album's radio hits included a version of Johnny Cash's "Cry, Cry, Cry" and the original compositions "'Til I Found You" and "Hillbilly Rock." The latter provided Stuart with his first top radio hit and now serves as his signature song.

By that time, Stuart had developed an individual stage style built around a huge personal collection of some 200 pieces of flashy cowboy clothes, which included dozens of jackets and shirts with special embroidery and rhinestone-studded patterns. He wanted to update the colorful western-styled attire of such country legends

as Hank Snow, Porter Wagoner, and Webb Pierce.

Stuart continued to write prolifically while establishing his own singing career, and his songs were recorded by such diverse performers as Mark Collie, Emmylou Harris, Buck Owens, and Jann Browne. Travis Tritt invited the colorful Stuart to join him in a duet of "The Whiskey Ain't Working," a song Stuart cowrote that became a top country hit in the first few weeks of 1992.

Stuart's next album, *Tempted*, kept the momentum of *Hillbilly Rock* rolling forward. Like *Hillbilly Rock*, this compelling collection was produced by Tony Brown and Richard Bennett, and it allowed the singer-instrumentalist to reveal his talent for bluegrass, honky tonk, and gospel as well as expanding on his country-rock style.

Above and above, left: Marty Stuart notched his first number-one country song in early 1992 with "The Whiskey Ain't Working," a duet with Travis Tritt. A colorful performer, Stuart owns more than 200 vintage country outfits, as well as a closetful of flashy, custom-made outfits that he calls his "work clothes." *Left:* A professional musician since the age of 12, Stuart has always enjoyed the support of his family, including his mother.

Pam Tillis, one of country music's hottest newcomers, isn't such a newcomer. The daughter of country great Mel Tillis, she appeared with him on the Grand Ole Opry—while it was still at the Ryman Auditorium—when she was just eight years old. During her musical career, she has moved from one label to another while experimenting with pop, rock, new wave, disco, and jazz before realizing that her roots in country music could not be ignored.

Above: Pam Tillis, daughter of veteran country star Mel Tillis, has been a successful songwriter in a variety of musical genres— even disco. But she has enjoyed her greatest success as a country singer and songwriter.

For years Tillis refused to listen to those who told her she was destined to follow in her father's footsteps. It was her own form of rebellion. The tales about her sleeping in her daddy's guitar case at a recording studio are true, but she claims that he was never around long enough to teach her how to play the instrument. When her parents divorced, Tillis admits that she was a troubled child.

When she was 16, Tillis was in a car accident that severely disfigured her face, requiring years of surgery. She eventually dropped out of the University of Tennessee and moved to San Francisco, where she formed a jazz-rock combo called Freeflight that became extremely popular in the Bay area. She married, then returned to Nashville in 1978, where her son, Ben, was born. Three weeks after his birth, she broke up with her husband.

Tillis earned a living as a session singer and songwriter. With her range of musical interests, Tillis's songs were recorded by such diverse performers as Juice Newton, Dan Seals, and r&b singer Chaka Khan. Even disco singer Gloria Gaynor recorded one of Tillis's tunes, "When I Get Around to It." Pam dreamed of a rock 'n' roll career though she continued to experiment with different musical styles. She fronted a top-40 r&b band for a while, eventually landing a record deal. Her first single, "Every Home Should Have One," was obviously influenced by the disco sounds of the 1970s, while her 1983 album *Above & Beyond the Doll of Cutey* represented her attempt at new wave.

Following a trip to England in the mid-1980s, Tillis returned to Nashville intent on exploring her country heritage. As a country singer and songwriter, she began making waves with

Above: Tillis confirmed her stardom with an enthusiastic performance of "Put Yourself in My Place" at the 1991 Country Music Association Awards show.

a string of solid singles. Songs penned by Tillis were recorded by Ricky Van Shelton and Highway 101, who took her "Someone Else's Trouble Now" to the top of the charts.

Signed to Arista Records in 1990, Tillis finally claimed her place as a country performer with the release of *Put Yourself in My Place*. Some claim the first single from that album, "Don't Tell Me What to Do," was the first debut record by a female country artist to hit number one in years. (Tillis had released records previously but not in the country music format.)

Tillis has collaborated with songwriter Bob DiPiero, a former member of the country band Billy Hill, on a number of tunes. On Valentine's Day in 1991, the two were married, making them collaborators personally as well as professionally.

Aaron Tippin muscled his way into country music with his first single, "You've Got to Stand for Something," a song that addressed America's need to vent emotions over the 1991 Persian Gulf conflict. That one tune was all it took for Bob Hope to take the muscular South Carolinian on a Middle East tour, where he performed alongside such other entertainers as Ann Jillian and Marie Osmond.

Tip, as he's called by friends, picked up his first guitar at the age of ten and tried his hand at songwriting a couple of years later. He started singing as a way to pass the time while he was driving a tractor, a fitting testament to his country upbringing.

Thanks in part to his rugged good looks and bodybuilder's physique, Aaron Tippin regularly receives flowers and other gifts during his personal appearances.

But, there's more to the 5'9" singer than his rural roots and South Carolina accent. Tippin earned his pilot's license by the time he was 15, and, at age 19, he was licensed to fly commercial multiengine aircraft. "When I was in high school, we owned a stunt plane," he recalls with a twinkle in his crisp blue eyes. "I didn't have to have a hot rod car—I had a hot rod airplane. So I terrorized the community—rode around upside-down and waved at everybody."

He intended to fly for a major airline, but the fuel shortage hit in the late 1970s. The airlines began furloughing pilots, not hiring new ones. With the "urban cowboy" craze in full swing, Tippin decided to devote his unflagging energies to music and was soon playing honky tonks on a steady basis. Inspired by Hank Williams, Jimmie Rodgers, Lefty Frizzell, Ernest Tubb, Hank Thompson, and Hank Snow, Tip fostered a hard-country style that made full use of his raw, distinctive voice—complete with a yodel here and there.

Around 1986, after the break-up of his marriage, he moved to Nashville, where his songwriting came to the attention of Charlie Monk at Opryland Music Group. Monk signed the enthusiastic Tippin to a writing contract. As he honed his skills as a tunesmith, he decided to concentrate on a career as a writer, not a performer, and was content to let artists such as Mark Collie, Charley Pride, Josh Logan, and the Kingsmen record his songs.

Though he wasn't pursuing a recording contract, Tippin's distinctive voice was heard around Nashville on the demo tapes he had made of his songs. Mary Martin, then an executive at RCA

Records, was looking for songs for another artist on the label when she heard an Aaron Tippin demo and realized his hard-driving honky tonk style deserved a wider audience. He reached that audience with his debut album, *You've Got to Stand for Something*, which included such Tippin songs as "I've Got a Good Memory" and "Ain't That a Hell of a Note."

As fans eagerly anticipate his second album, Tippin promises it will be as exciting as the first. "When I turn in a project to RCA, I ain't afraid to put a blindfold on 'em, stick the titles on the wall, and let 'em stick their finger on anyone they want to. I don't believe in a couple of singles and whatever else is handy. Folks pay too much money for this stuff nowadays, and they deserve nothing but the best."

Tippin is naturally pleased with his success but has to laugh about the reaction of his teenage daughter, Charla, after he phoned her to say he'd landed a record deal. Though pleased, Charla wasn't as enthusiastic as Tippin had hoped; it seems she was more concerned at the moment with getting her dad's permission to enter a beauty pageant.

RANDY TRAVIS

Minnie Pearl, country music's most famous humorist, once described Randy Travis as "a new vehicle with old wheels." She meant he sounded good, he looked good, and he was moving country music into the future by relying on the musical styles of the past. It was a high compliment from a colorful lady who had worked alongside the greatest country music singers of all time. She underlined her feelings about Travis's talents by adding, "A voice like his only comes along once in a generation."

Above: Randy Travis cast the mold for the new kind of country music star that has surfaced since the late 1980s. He's handsome, humble, business-minded, and loyal to the roots of country music. *Opposite:* Travis's formal introduction to the guitar came at age eight, when he began to take lessons from Kate Mangum in New Salem, North Carolina.

Travis turned the country music world around in 1986, the year he became Nashville's biggest overnight sensation in history. *Storms of Life*, his debut album on Warner Bros. Records, ranks as the first debut album by a country music artist to sell more than one million copies within a year of its release.

It's important to note that Travis's success came when country music sales were at a low point after steadily decreasing for several years. John Anderson, Ricky Skaggs, George Strait, and the Judds had already sent ripples of optimism through the industry by swimming against the flow of pop-influenced, cosmopolitan country music coming out of Nashville in the early 1980s. The meteoric success of Travis turned the tide completely, opening the gates for the flood of successful traditional performers that followed.

Like most overnight sensations, Travis spent several hardworking years paying his dues before getting his big break. The second of six children, Randy Traywick was born May 4, 1959, in the small North Carolina town of Marshville, about 30 miles from Charlotte in an area known as the Piedmont Crescent. His father, Harold Traywick, bred horses, raised turkeys, and managed a small construction firm. His mother, Bobbie Traywick, worked in a fabric mill sorting pot holders.

At age eight, Travis began to diligently learn chords on an acoustic guitar. Two years later, his father dressed his four eager sons in western suits, gave them all acoustic guitars, and pressed them into service as a country

Randy Travis married his longtime manager, Lib Hatcher, on May 31, 1991, in a private ceremony on the Hawaiian island of Maui. At the time of their marriage, the two had been business associates for 14 years.

Right: Travis and Lib Hatcher opened the Randy Travis Souvenirs & Gifts Shop on Demonbreun Street in Nashville in May of 1989. The shop features personal mementos and souvenirs with the singer's name and likeness.

singing, she knew that this skinny 17-year-old could be a star. He won the contest, and Hatcher introduced herself afterward, inquiring about his life. With the consent of his parents, she appealed to the court to put him on probation and in her care. Travis moved in with Hatcher and her husband and took over as vocalist at Country City USA. The club manager dedicated herself to grooming the young roustabout. She devoted so much time to him that her husband eventually gave her an ultimatum: Sell the club and tell the singer to move out. She chose otherwise, and her husband left her and filed for divorce.

In 1978, singer Joe Stampley heard Travis sing and offered his help. Stampley produced a handful of songs, four of which were released under the name of Randy Traywick on an independent label, Paula Records. Stampley also took tapes of the songs back to

harmony act known as the Traywick Brothers. Even then, his folks said, the young boy had a voice that drew attention.

By the time he reached his teens, Travis was veering into trouble. He dropped out of school before finishing the ninth grade. He immersed himself in a life of fast cars, hard drinking, and recreational drug use. His initial scrape with the police included a 100-mile-an-hour car chase, culminating with Travis losing control and spinning into an open field. Trouble continued until he was arrested for breaking and entering, a felony with a potential jail sentence of five years.

Before his court date, the troubled youngster signed up for a talent contest at Country City USA, Charlotte's pre-eminent country music honky tonk. The club was managed and partly owned by Lib Hatcher. She remembers dropping a load of papers she was carrying the first time she heard Travis's voice. She stopped what she was doing and listened. By the time he finished

Nashville and presented them to several record companies, but no one showed any interest.

Hatcher and her protegé weren't ready to give up. In 1980, Hatcher sold her nightclub, and the two moved to Nashville. They rented one floor of a three-story, yellow-brick building on 16th Avenue in an area known as Music Row, where most of the Nashville music industry is located. On the ground floor were the offices of the trade magazine *Radio & Records*. For a while, Travis swept and scrubbed the offices once a week for a $30 fee.

Hatcher talked her way into a job managing the Nashville Palace, a tourist-oriented music club and restaurant located in a strip of shops directly across from the entrance to the Opryland Hotel. Travis went to work with her, mopping floors and flipping

Since the late 1980s, Travis has earned more than $10 million annually in concert fees. In addition, his merchandising company earns millions more selling everything from conventional items like T-shirts to more creative products, such as Randy Travis notebooks and coloring books.

hamburgers. He also sang when he could, performing under his new stage name, Randy Ray. At first, he'd sneak in a few songs at the invitation of the nightly headliner. Eventually, he worked himself into a full-time slot, leading the band five nights a week, three sets a night.

Hatcher continued to scheme: She instigated a night featuring performances by stars of the Grand Ole Opry, allowing Travis an opportunity to meet and mingle with several of Nashville's well-traveled veterans. She enthusiastically invited everyone and anyone involved with the recording industry to visit the club, enjoy a free meal, and see the featured singer. Through the early 1980s, every record company in Nashville turned down a chance to sign Randy Travis. Not once, but twice. Record executives were leery of his

unabashedly country style, and he had no inclination to change it toward a more pop-flavored sound. The list of those who passed on Travis included Warner Bros. Records.

However, Martha Sharp had yet to hear or see the Palace star. The top talent executive at Warner Bros., Sharp finally accepted an invitation from Hatcher in 1985. The singer was grilling steaks when Sharp arrived and requested to hear him. Hatcher hurried into the kitchen and told him to get onstage, and she'd turn the steaks.

Sharp knew that night she wanted to sign Travis to a record contract. She also knew she would have a hard time convincing her superiors to believe in a singer so obviously devoted to traditional sounding country music. Despite confronting strong doubts, she succeeded.

Sharp introduced Travis to Kyle Lehning, an accomplished engineer who had worked with Ronnie Milsap and was moving into record production. Lehning produced most of what became Travis's breakthrough album, *Storms of Life* (two songs were produced by Keith Stegall). Before releasing the album, however, Warner Bros. wanted to test the reaction to Travis's music on radio. The first single, "On the Other Hand," received a disappointing initial reaction, climbing to only number 67 on the country charts. The next song, "1982," fared better, breaking Travis into the top ten. Warner Bros., in an unusual move, gave "On the Other Hand" another chance. This time the tune climbed to number one, a position Travis would visit many a times in the

Travis, pictured here with George Jones and Mark Chesnutt, has cited Jones as one of his primary heroes and influences. The two recorded a duet for Travis's *Heroes and Friends* discs in 1990 and starred in a Home Box Office cable special a year later.

Opposite: Travis grew up with horses and still enjoys spending his leisure time grooming and riding thoroughbreds. His personal stable includes a descendant of Roy Rogers's late, great Trigger, and a quarter horse, Platinum Harry, that was a gift from Warner Bros. Records.

next five years. *Storms of Life*, in addition to its record-setting sales pace, spent 12 weeks at number one.

With his second album, *Always and Forever,* Travis sealed his status as a country superstar. The album spawned four consecutive number-one songs—"Forever and Ever, Amen," "I Won't Need You Anymore," "Too Gone, Too Long," and "I Told You So"—and spent an astounding ten months atop the country album sales chart. Along the way, he set the mold for the country star of the late 20th century. He's clean-cut and square-jawed. He dresses in a crisp, casual style with creases in his jeans, starch in his shirt, and a western tone to the cut of his jackets. Nothing too gaudy or flashy, and nary a rhinestone in sight. He's humble, compliant, and reverent toward the stars who preceded him. He's a teetotaler who monitors his diet. He sings with uncontrived sincerity, and his lower register features a warmth and breadth that brings a mournfulness to all of his work.

Travis dominated the awards shows during the late 1980s, winning more than 40 honors in his first four years. He won a Grammy for best country vocal performance by a male as well as several awards from the Country Music Association and the Academy of Country Music. His albums—*Old 8 x 10, No Holdin' Back, Heroes and Friends*—extended his million-selling streak into the 1990s. Travis has also inspired younger performers to stick close to their roots in their music. In doing so, he changed the course of country music.

Travis Tritt burst on the country music scene in late 1989 with his first single, "Country Club," and provided a new anthem for the working-class man. He also provided female fans with something—the latest, long-haired, sexy-looking country idol.

The bearded singer lauded the working-class lifestyle in his "Country Club" video, making it an instant success. The song and video assured country listeners that it was okay to shoot pool rather than play golf, drink beer rather than champagne, drive a pickup instead of a Mercedes, and go two-stepping instead of dirty dancing.

Above: Travis Tritt accepted a platinum record for his *It's All About to Change* album. Marty Stuart and Charlie Daniels were on hand to celebrate Tritt's hard-won success. *Opposite:* Tritt has stayed true to the personal beliefs that echo in his music.

"Country Club" reinforced a familiar philosophy in country music: Pretention is out; having a raucous good time is in. It's a philosophy that suits James Travis Tritt perfectly.

Born February 9, 1963, in Marietta, Georgia, Tritt grew up on his family's 40-acre farm. The family surname is a derivation of Trittendorf, a German appellation. His father, James, supplemented the family income by working as a bread-truck driver, auto mechanic, and school bus driver. Tritt's mother, Gwen, passed on to her son her religious beliefs, encouraging him to sing in their church's children's choir.

Tritt developed a love of music as a young boy and taught himself to play the guitar when he was only eight years

old. By the time he was 14, he was writing songs. His parents, particularly his father, tried to instill in him a pragmatic, self-sufficient work ethic by discouraging his musical aspirations. Undaunted, he pressed on, and his relationship with his parents turned rocky.

The family's stability was hindered by James and Gwen's divorce when Tritt was 15. Even after they reunited and were remarried three years later, their headstrong son had difficulty making his father understand his dream. When he got married three months after graduating from high school, it was basically just to get out of the house, away from the constant bickering. His bride was against his musical

Tritt once faced opposition from his family over his choice of a career. But now mother Gwen, father James, and sister Sheila wouldn't have him do anything else.

ambitions. Not surprisingly, the marriage ended in less than two years.

Tritt did exhibit some of his father's work ethic in spite of their many disagreements. For four years, he supported himself by working at a heating and air conditioning firm, starting on the loading docks and working his way up to assistant manager. But a talk with his boss convinced him to give music a shot. "He had been a rock 'n' roller and at one time had the opportunity to lay everything aside and go play music—and he didn't do it," Tritt told the *Chicago Tribune*. "He's in his forties now and very successful financially, but he kicks himself every day for not pursuing his dream."

For six months, the hard-working singer continued his day job and then performed in clubs at night. Pushed to the point of exhaustion and realizing that steady employment as a musician was possible, he quit his job at the heating and air conditioning company. His resignation caused a serious repercussion—his father stopped speaking to him.

By 1984, Tritt was making a meager living as a club act across Georgia, and he married again. This time, wife Jodi Barnett believed in his dream, acting as his manager, his consultant, and his booking agent. She eventually became so wrapped up in his career that she lost her own identity. When Tritt landed a record deal, professionals stepped in and took over the responsibilities she had handled. It was the beginning of their breakup, and they divorced in 1989.

Tritt's professional break came when he met Danny Davenport, a local pop promotion man for Warner Bros. Records, in 1984. Davenport allowed Tritt to use his home recording studio, offering guidance to the aspiring singer-songwriter. Over the next two years, they worked together and recorded enough songs for an album. When enough Warner Bros. executives heard the project, Tritt finally landed a record deal in 1988.

Because the label already had one Travis (Randy), they urged Tritt to change his name and offered suggestions such as James Parrish, Nick Tritt, James Hunter, and even his given name, James Tritt. Much to the relief of the young singer, label executives finally allowed him to remain Travis Tritt.

Recruiting Ken Kragen as his manager was another milestone. Kragen, who manages superstar Kenny Rogers and who was the driving force behind the recordings of "We Are the World" and "Hands Across America," had refused to handle an entry level act for more than 20 years. He changed his mind when he recognized Tritt's promise as a future superstar.

Tritt's debut album, *Country Club*, showcased his versatility with such diverse songs as the boisterous Southern rock anthem "Put Some Drive in Your Country," the unabashedly country song "Drift Off to Dream," and the heartrending ballad "Help Me Hold On." The album was an immediate best-seller and was certified gold in September 1990, just six months after its release. In July 1991, it was certified platinum.

The success of *Country Club* resulted in a nomination for the Country Music Association's coveted Horizon Award in 1990. Though he lost the award to Garth Brooks, he managed to snag it the next year. Tritt was so delighted at winning the Horizon Award that he blurted out at the backstage press conference, "I'm so excited I'm just about to wet my pants."

In addition to the nominations and accolades, success brought about an even greater reward. Tritt's fractured relationship with his parents was mended when the elder Tritt realized his son had made the right choice.

It's All About to Change, Tritt's second album, contained more of the singer's high-energy style of country music. Not part of the neo-traditionalists, who dominated country music in the early 1990s, Tritt has been influenced more by Hank Williams, Jr., than by Hank Williams. "Here's a Quarter (Call Someone Who Cares)" propelled album sales to gold status, while his next single, "Anymore," shot to the top of the charts and hurtled album sales to platinum level. Other noteworthy tunes from his collection included "If Hell Had a Jukebox" and "Bible Belt."

Tritt's popularity was acknowledged by the music industry when he received two Grammy nominations (best male country vocal performance and best country song for "Here's a Quarter") in January 1992.

Tritt and "hillbilly rocker" Marty Stuart struck up a professional relationship and personal friendship when they met at Fan Fair—an annual gathering in which country stars greet their fans—in the summer of 1991. The duo recorded a rowdy single together called "The Whiskey Ain't Workin'," which climbed to the top of the charts. The pairing of Tritt and Stuart was overwhelmingly successful, and the duo embarked on their "No Hats" tour at the end of 1991. An in-joke in the music industry, the tour's title comes from the pair's refusal to be grouped with such neo-traditionalists as Alan Jackson and Clint Black who are noted for their trademark hats.

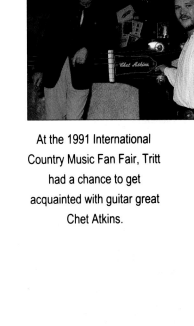

At the 1991 International Country Music Fan Fair, Tritt had a chance to get acquainted with guitar great Chet Atkins.

A versatile singer, Tritt can belt out a country anthem, then throttle back for an emotional ballad. Although mindful of the roots of country music and the "traditional" sound, Tritt has chosen not to link himself with Clint Black and other "new traditionalists."

TANYA TUCKER

In 1972, Tanya Tucker came roaring into county music like a Texas tornado with her first single, "Delta Dawn." Fans enjoyed her lusty vocals but were shocked to discover that the husky, sensual voice belonged to a 13 year old.

While industry insiders considered her overnight success at such an early age a head start on a promising career, Tucker would later remark that she felt she had started a little late. After all, she knew she wanted a career in music when she was just eight years old, and by the age of nine, she and her family were already making plans and setting goals.

Above: Besides being one of the most talented and energetic of all country stars, Tanya Tucker may also be the most controversial. Early in her career, she cultivated a powerful sex appeal. *Opposite:* Later, Tucker adopted a more traditional persona. Either way, she's an exciting talent.

Born in Seminole, Texas, Tucker was encouraged as a young child to pursue her dream by her parents, Juanita and Beau (who now serves as her manager). In fact, Beau drove his ambitious daughter to Nashville from their home in Wilcox, Arizona, when she was nine so she could get a first-hand look at the home of country music. Later, they arranged for her to audition for the movie *Jeremiah Johnson*, which starred Robert Redford. She landed a small role in the 1972 film—a bit of trivia unknown to many of her fans.

After the family relocated to Henderson, Nevada (near Las Vegas), Beau Tucker financed a demo tape for

his ambitious, young daughter. The tape eventually reached producer Billy Sherrill. Impressed by her vocal strength and maturity, Sherrill signed her to Columbia Records.

The confident teenager felt strongly about the type of material she wanted to record for her debut album. Sherrill introduced her to a song he considered a sure-fire hit, "Happiest Girl in the Whole USA." Tucker turned it down with no hesitation. The song eventually became a hit for its cowriter Donna Fargo, but, in retrospect, the tune's bland pop style and syrupy lyrics indicate that Tucker's hesitation about recording it was justified. Tucker

Right: An ill-starred engagement to singer Glen Campbell put Tucker in the spotlight, and made her a darling of tabloid journalists.

Tucker has delighted in pushing country music fashions to the limit, from the ultra-sexy to the wild and woolly.

picked a winner on her own, "Delta Dawn," which resulted in her first hit record. Tucker proved that her initial success was not due to the novelty of her age by recording other hit songs, including "Jamestown Ferry," "What's Your Mama's Name," and "Blood Red & Goin' Down." Tucker became identified with a certain type of song in which a dramatic story about the harsh side of life was conveyed through her powerhouse vocal style.

By the time she reached her 16th birthday, the sultry teenager had become a sophisticated and successful performer with a string of top-ten albums: *Delta Dawn, What's Your Mama's Name, Would You Lay with Me (In a Field of Stone), Tanya Tucker,* and *Lovin' and Learnin'.* She also racked up a considerable number of top-ten hits, including "Lizzie & the Rainman" and "San Antonio Stroll."

In addition to becoming one of country music's hottest singers, she also gained a reputation as a hard-living free

spirit. Cancelling almost $1 million in concert dates in 1978, Tucker moved to Los Angeles and repackaged herself as a spandex-clad siren for her *TNT* album, which pushed her style toward rock 'n' roll. Although the album, which featured the hit "Texas (When I Die)," was another best-seller, the move backfired. Her career slowly fizzled, extinguished in part by her widely publicized tendency to walk on the wild side. "I was the wildest thing out there," Tucker told *People* magazine in 1988. "I could stay up longer, drink more...I was on the ragged edge."

She also experienced a series of well-publicized romances, which added to her sex kitten image. By the time she was 24, she had been involved with actor Don Johnson, country legend Merle Haggard, pop singer Andy Gibb, and singer Glen Campbell. She blames her turbulent relationship and subsequent breakup with Campbell on the difference in their ages. She was 22 when the 44-year-old Campbell gave her an engagement ring, which is still in her possession.

Other problems followed the much-publicized breakup. By 1982, after spending her last $7,500 on a friend's cancer treatment, Tucker was broke. Backtracking from her pop-rock image, she released two solid country singles, "Pecos Promenade" and "Can I See You Tonight," which became top-ten hits.

Following a three-year break from recording, Tucker signed with Capitol Records in 1986. Her first Capitol album, *Girls Like Me,* marked a return to the same distinctive, melodic vocals that had made her a star 14 years earlier. She ended her dry spell on the charts with "One Love at a Time," "I'll Come Back as Another Woman," and "Just Another Love." Tucker reclaimed her position as one of country's leading ladies with her 1987 album, *Love Me Like You Used To*. Several successful singles from the album, including "I Won't Take Less Than Your Love" (recorded with Paul Davis and Paul Overstreet), "If It Don't Come Easy," and the title tune, resulted in two Country Music Association nominations in 1988. She was nominated for vocal collaboration and as female vocalist of the year. She would be nominated for the female vocalist award for the next three years.

Although her career was back on track, the dynamic singer battled more personal problems in 1988. Confronted by her family, she checked into the Betty Ford Clinic for six weeks to overcome alcohol and cocaine addictions. "My problem mainly was just a matter of boredom on the road and the loneliness," she told *USA Today*. "You get applause and admiration, and then you're back in the hotel room by yourself."

Fiercely independent, Tucker made headlines in 1989 when she gave birth to her daughter, Presley Tanita (named after Elvis Presley). Announcing her intention to remain unmarried and raise Presley by herself, she declined to name the baby's father at that time. As she celebrated her daughter's birth, she expanded as an artist. After the release of the softer, uncluttered *Strong Enough to Bend*, produced by longtime friend and supporter Jerry Crutchfield, Tucker delivered a *Greatest Hits* album.

The following year, she released *Tennessee Woman*, which featured the hits "Don't Go Out" (with T. Graham Brown), "Walking Shoes," "It Won't Be Me," and "Oh, What It Did to Me."

With her 1991 album, *What Do I Do with Me*, Tucker seemed firmly established as one of Music City's most dependable hitmakers. In addition to turning out such radio-friendly tunes as "Down to My Last Teardrop," Tucker, an excellent horsewoman, found time to win the National Cutting Horse Assocation's Third Annual Futurity Celebrity Cutting Championship. It wasn't the only prize she took home in 1991. On October 2, she was a double winner, giving birth to a son, Beau Grayson, just hours before being named CMA's female vocalist of the year.

Not content to rest on her laurels, Tucker looks ahead to more hit records. She reflects on her highly public professional and personal life with a grin and muses, "If I'd done half the things people say, I'd be dead."

By 1992, Tucker's life was perfectly on track. After receiving a gold record for her *What Do I Do With Me* album, she celebrated with daughter Presley and son Beau.

Ricky Van Shelton was once a dyed-in-the-wool rock 'n' roll fan, who had no desire to be a country singer. One night, his brother Ronnie asked Shelton to grab his guitar and join him and his bluegrass band for a gig. Ricky wasn't at all inclined to go along until Ronnie told him that he could drive. It wasn't just any car that convinced the 14-year-old that he should join the band—it was Ronnie's 1964 Ford Fairlane 289.

Right: His success the product of talent and plenty of hard work, Ricky Van Shelton has dominated fan polls with his infectious updating of the rockabilly and honky tonk styles.

The teenager soon realized that he wasn't going along just because he got to drive. He actually liked the music they were playing, and he began to listen to such classic country artists as Hank Williams and the Osborne Brothers. Over the next several years, he performed country music for audiences wherever he could find them—at fish fries, local clubs, even in his friends' living rooms. To avoid confusion with another Ricky Shelton who lived in the area (they kept getting each other's mail), he added his middle name—Van—hoping that his mail would be delivered to his mailbox. It wasn't long before his friends started to call him Ricky Van.

Despite having to work hard most of his life, the handsome Virginian always managed to devote time to his songwriting, a pastime he enjoyed even before he developed an interest in country music. He worked up his first song, a slow rocker called "My Conscience Is Bothering Me," on the guitar when he was 13.

Always believing that he could make a living with his music, Shelton honed his skills by performing as often as possible. Consumed by his music, his social life was limited. In fact, he once joked that his primary date was a guitar, though he did find time to meet his future wife, Bettye. The two were married in 1980.

Bettye realized her husband could never have the career he wanted if they stayed in Grit, Virginia. She found a job in Nashville so he could pursue his dream. But months later, after trying to generate interest from record labels, Shelton was no closer to stardom than

he had been in Grit. Once again, Bettye was able to help her husband out. One of her coworkers gave Shelton's homemade demo tape to her husband, Jerry Thompson, a respected columnist for Nashville's morning paper, *The Tennessean*. A friend of Thompson's, Rick Blackburn, happened to be the head of CBS Records at the time. At Thompson's urging, Blackburn agreed to attend a showcase of Shelton's in June 1986. Accompanied by producer

The mere sound of Van Shelton's deep Virginia drawl is enough to send many of his fans into swoons.

Steve Buckingham, Blackburn knew he'd found a star.

Shelton's professional career took off quickly. Within two weeks of his showcase, he was in the studio recording his first album, *Wild Eyed Dream*, with Buckingham serving as producer. Buckingham and Shelton proved a magical combination as the two selected songs written by some of Nashville's most respected tunesmiths, including Harlan Howard, Roger Miller, Buck Owens, and Merle Haggard. "Crime of Passion" was the second single from the album, and it soared into the top ten. The follow-up tune, "Somebody Lied," became the first of many number one records for Shelton. He was honored to appear on the Grand Ole

In 1991 Van Shelton teamed with Dolly Parton for a hit record, "Rockin' Year." The video that resulted was the year's number one clip on Country Music Television.

Opry in June 1987 and was so enthusiastically applauded that he was called back for an encore—a rare occurrence on the Opry stage.

Wild Eyed Dream delivered Shelton at his best, from his aching, dramatic treatment of the ballad "Life Turned Her That Way" to his rip-roaring command of such rocking tunes as "Ultimately Fine" and "Crazy over You." Not surprisingly, the album went to the top of the charts and was certified platinum.

For Shelton, 1988 was a year he'll always remember as it brought him a slew of awards. He was named top new male vocalist by the Academy of Country Music, the Music City News star of tomorrow, and winner of the

Country Music Association's Horizon Award. The soft-spoken singer also became a member of the Grand Ole Opry that year. Just eight weeks after the release of his second album, *Loving Proof*, Shelton had another gold album to add to his collection. *Loving Proof*, like its predecessor, was a best-seller and was eventually certified platinum.

Shelton has dominated the fan-voted awards in recent years. In 1989, he claimed three TNN Viewers Choice trophies and four Music City News awards, including best male vocalist from both organizations. When TNN and Music City News combined their awards shows in 1990, fans voted him both male vocalist and Entertainer of the Year. The following year, he took home the same awards. At a backstage press conference, he told the media, "I know where my bread is buttered. Without the fans, I wouldn't be here. An award that's given to me by the fans is more important than any other, and you can take that to the bank."

Shelton's third album, *RVS III*, continued the same mix of the old and the new, the honky tonk music and the rockabilly that characterized his other work. With *RVS III*, the singer also enjoyed a similar rate of success, producing four top-five hits—"Statue of a Fool" (a number-one remake of the Jack Greene classic), "I've Cried My Last Tear for You," "I Meant Every Word He Said," and "Life's Little Ups & Downs." Like his two previous albums, this best-seller was certified platinum. The talented singer-songwriter followed up with *Backroads* in 1991, another collection of tunes demonstrating his rich, powerful country voice. Aside from indicating that Shelton was equally at home with a rocking backbeat or a soaring ballad, *Backroads* ventured into new territory with Shelton's duet with country superstar Dolly Parton. "Rockin' Years" became a chart-topper, which was accompanied by a music video eventually named CMT's number-one video of 1991.

Combining his humble manner and rich Virginia drawl with a lifelong dedication to country music, Shelton has become one of the most beloved entertainers in the United States. He has landed a coveted spot in the hearts of country fans that is the envy of other entertainers. "Walking on stage is still the best," he believes. "I love the music, I love the people yelling and screaming. That's where I'm happiest."

Much of Van Shelton's enormous success can be attributed to the diversity of his material. He can rock the house down with a classic like "Great Balls of Fire," or tickle the ladies with a love song like "Loving Proof."

Combine a smooth singing style with Southern manners and you end up with one of country music's most popular performers. Van Shelton's fans can't get enough of him.

Hank Williams, Jr., performed his first concert at the tender age of eight. He recorded his first song at 14. He scored his first major country song at age 16. But, as suggested by the title and lyrics of his second hit, "Standin' in the Shadows," the young man who had changed his name from Randall Hank Williams to Hank Williams, Jr., was quite aware that he was riding the coattails of his legendary father. Hank, Sr., died from the effects of hard living in 1953, leaving behind a haunting legacy for his three-year-old son.

Both pages: Hank Williams, Jr., like many of his Southern rock brethren, enthusiastically expresses his appreciation for the United States. His patriotic fervor is just one indication of his upbeat nature—a mindset that undoubtedly helped him to overcome massive injuries suffered in a near-fatal fall in 1975.

Hank, Jr., spent the 1960s performing his father's songs, adhering to his mother's career direction, and indulging a growing appetite for drugs and alcohol. In 1974, Williams decided to step out of his father's long shadow and stand on his own. Against the wishes of his mother, Audrey Williams, he moved from Nashville to Cullman, Alabama, initiated a divorce from his second wife, and began an album that combined Southern rock, Delta blues, and rebel country.

Williams celebrated the completion of this new, ground-breaking collection of songs by going on a hunting and hiking trip in Montana. During an outing, he suffered massive head injuries when he slipped on a ledge and fell 500 feet down a jagged, rocky slope of Mount Ajax. He underwent several operations to reconstruct his face over the next eight months. Adding to the stress of his rehabilitation was the death of his mother three months after his fall.

While the singer recuperated, the landmark *Hank Williams & Friends* album was released. It was a bold departure for Williams and featured contributions from country rock performers such as Charlie Daniels, Toy Caldwell of the Marshall Tucker Band, and Chuck Leavell of the Allman Brothers. The album's rock edges alienated Williams from the Nashville establishment and from his longtime record company, MGM Records. The album included the song "Living Proof," a

Vintage Williams, seen here performing with his band at L.A.'s famous Palomino Club in the late 1970s. Since that period, Williams has been packing big-capacity auditoriums and arenas.

Right: Williams and his son Shelton display two recent awards, including one for the prestigious Entertainer of the Year, presented by the Academy of Country Music.

lament about a drunkard taunting Hank, Jr., that he would never be as good as his father. Williams later adopted it as the title of his 1979 autobiography, which was then turned into a made-for-television movie starring Richard Thomas as the colorful singer.

Williams proved how well he had recovered by releasing *The New South* in 1977, a pointed statement about his vision of a new musical style. Produced by Waylon Jennings, *The New South* was Williams's first album after joining the new record company established by music industry mogul Mike Curb. This album began an association with Curb/Warner Bros. that would last until 1992. Williams closed the 1970s by setting several personal sales records. He released the *Family Tradition* album in April and followed it with *Whiskey Bent and Hellbound* in October. Both albums topped 500,000 in sales within a year. Thirty years after his birth on May 26,

1949, in Shreveport, Louisiana, Williams had succeeded in forging his own identity. Manager and close friend Merle Kilgore declared via song that he wasn't going to call Williams "Junior" anymore, which was his way of acknowledging Hank, Jr.'s, new, unique style.

By 1982, Williams had attracted a fanatically loyal following. In concert, he regularly drew crowds of 10,000 or more fans, a rarity for a country music artist at that time. And, he continued to pull in those numbers for the remainder of the decade. In October 1982, the nine albums he had created in the previous five years ranked on *Billboard* magazine's Top Country Albums chart—a record-breaking accomplishment that stands unequalled. (The albums were *One Night Stand*, *The New South*, *Family Tradition*, *Whiskey Bent and Hellbound*, *Habits Old and New*, *Rowdy*, *The Pressure Is On*, *High Notes*, and *Hank Williams Jr.'s Greatest Hits*.) By the end

of the 1980s, Williams's total sales topped the $25 million mark. Despite his success, Williams was shunned by the various country-music awards organizations. He was viewed as more of an outsider than even country outlaws Waylon Jennings and Willie Nelson. His open criticism of Nashville's recording and business practices had apparently hurt him within the tight-knit Music City community.

Eventually, the country music industry began to come around. In 1985, Williams received a video of the year award from the Country Music Association for the raucous "All My Rowdy Friends Are Coming over Tonight." When accepting the trophy, he quipped, "You know, I make a little audio, too."

Two years later, Williams began to gain the recognition that seemed so long overdue. The Academy of Country Music kicked off his big year by naming him Entertainer of the Year, and a few months later, the CMA granted him their version of that same honor. The CMA also gave the video of the year award to his video version of "My Name Is Bocephus." In 1988, he was again named Entertainer of the Year by both country music organizations, and *Born to Boogie* was designated album of the year by the CMA. In 1989, he received the CMA's award for vocal event of the year for his hit "There's a Tear in My Beer," a high-tech duet recording that combined Williams's voice with a newly discovered, long-lost audio track of Hank, Sr. He also won an award for the video rendition of the song, which used special effects to place the younger Williams into old film footage of the senior Williams in performance. In 1990, Hank, Jr., won his first Grammy Award for the same father-son vocal duet.

Meanwhile, Williams's music was introduced to the mainstream audience in a unique way when "All my Rowdy Friends Are Coming Over Tonight" became the theme song for *Monday Night Football* on ABC-TV. In 1991, he rewrote the song as "*Monday Night Football Boogie*" especially for the program.

The pervasive influence of Williams's introduction of a rock sound to country music became apparent in the late 1980s with the success of the Kentucky HeadHunters, Travis Tritt, Pirates of the Mississippi, and others. Williams championed the youthful new sound with his hit song "Young Country" in 1988, and he has served as an elder statesman of progressive country music to the newcomers.

The singer continues to be an avid outdoorsman, retreating for a period each year to a 300-acre spread in Montana to hunt big game and fish. He even moved his business office to Paris, Tennessee, which is located in an area suitable for outdoor recreation. As the last decade of the 20th century moves forward, Williams continues to make changes and grow. In 1990, he married his fourth wife, Mary Jane Thomas. The following year, he terminated several long-running business associations when he switched his concert bookings to the William Morris Agency and signed a multiyear recording contract with Capricorn Records.

A true artist with a long career in front of him, Williams has already made his mark on country music.

The Hank Williams, Jr. Museum, owned by Williams, offers fans a chance to look through the singer's memorabilia. Included among the exhibits is the Cadillac in which Williams's father died while riding to a Canton, Ohio, concert on New Year's Day, 1953.

TRISHA YEARWOOD

In the late 1980s, Garth Brooks made Trisha Yearwood a promise. If he got a break in the recording industry, he would do everything he could to help her. She pledged a similar pact with him.

At the time, the talents of these two were unknown outside a circle of music publishers and songwriters on Nashville's Music Row. But within that crowd, Brooks and Yearwood had acquired reputations as strong, forceful vocalists who worked fast and who breathed life into songs. The two were hired regularly by songwriters and music publishers for "demo sessions," in which new songs are put on tapes for presentation to recording artists, producers, and record companies in hopes someone will choose the songs for an upcoming album.

Above: Trisha Yearwood diligently worked her way up the music-business ladder, starting as an intern at a record company and ending up a star. *Opposite:* Although Yearwood had plenty of singing experience before recording her first album, she had done little singing before live audiences. After just a few months of live dates, she had crafted a polished, confident stage show.

Meanwhile, producer Garth Fundis took an interest in Yearwood's potential. He helped her choose and record a few songs, then sent the tapes to Nashville record executives. MCA Records signed her to a recording contract after seeing her perform at a Nashville nightclub.

When Brooks heard the news, he kept his promise. He set Yearwood up with his management team, Bob Doyle and Pam Lewis. He invited her to perform as his opening act during the sec-

ond half of 1991, making her a part of the biggest country music tour at the time. He also sent out his endorsement in writing—"Trisha could sell oil to the Arabs with her voice," Brooks said in an MCA press release that went out with Yearwood's first song.

Yearwood's first hit, "She's in Love with the Boy," didn't need much assistance. A catchy story of formative young love, the hit pushed its way up the charts. Some claim that it was the first debut single by a female artist in

Yearwood earned a coveted performance slot on the Country Music Association Awards show in October 1991. Although a newcomer to the record charts, she joined such major stars as Reba McEntire and Garth Brooks.

26 years to reach number one on the country music charts. (these claims vary according to the source).

Her album, *Trisha Yearwood*, produced by Fundis and released in July 1991, sold more than 500,000 copies within three months. The album included two songs cowritten by Brooks, including the second hit, "Like We Never Made a Broken Heart," an honest, unsentimental picture of a one-night stand featuring Brooks on harmony. Yearwood also recorded Brooks's "Victim of the Game," which he cowrote with Pat Alger.

The initial sales boom marked a meteoric takeoff for the tall young woman from a small Georgia town who confessed she was intimidated when she first arrived in Nashville in 1985. She grew up in Monticello, a village of about 2,000 people some 60 miles from Atlanta. "I'm basically a country girl," she noted. "My mom and dad have jobs, but we live on a farm."

Her earliest memories of singing involve the time a neighbor presented her with a stack of Elvis Presley records. She started singing along with everything, she recalled. She sang along with her parents' country albums, the Southern rock on the radio, and especially cassettes of the Eagles and Linda Ronstadt, whom Yearwood tabs as her primary influence because of the strength and emotional resonance of her voice. Her first performance experiences came in high school musicals and choral groups.

She enrolled at the University of Georgia after high school, but her studies convinced her that her heart belonged to music. With the support of her parents, she transferred to Nashville's Belmont University and signed up for the music business curriculum. Life in a bigger city required some adjustment. "I wasn't used to going to a gas station and not having somebody ask me about my grades or how my mom and dad were," she remembered. "I wasn't used to going into the grocery store and not having to plan on staying to catch up with everybody and tell them how I was doing."

While attaining her degree at Belmont, she began working as an intern in the publicity department at MTM Records. After graduation, she returned to the firm as a receptionist.

The work sharpened her knowledge of the music industry and introduced her to many movers and shakers.

Before long, Yearwood was singing on demo sessions, following a path to stardom taken by Janie Fricke, Kathy Mattea, Holly Dunn, Joe Diffie, Billy Dean, and many others. She also met Chris Latham, an employee at the publishing firm of EMI Music, who became her husband.

Yearwood also confronted a bias many ambitious female performers encounter when starting a career in country music. She was told not to set her expectations too high, that few opportunities were open for women, and even fewer women achieve record sales equal to the top male stars. Women buy most records, she was told, and they aren't as enthusiastic about performers of the same gender.

With Reba McEntire as her inspiration, Yearwood planned to prove otherwise. She purposefully chose songs representing a woman's point of view. She passed over songs about "weak women" who forgive too easily, while searching for songs about strong women with high self-worth. Yearwood's gutsy version of "That's What I Like About You"—written for a man who lists the attributes he likes in the opposite sex—gives the song a different spin and turns the stereotypes around.

Yearwood has displayed a comparable boldness in her personal and business affairs. She split from her husband in the fall of 1991, stating their relationship had been rocky for two years and her constant traveling made it impossible to work out their problems. She also changed management just as her career

started to skyrocket, signing on with Los Angeles-based Ken Kragen, manager of Kenny Rogers and Travis Tritt.

She has flashed her aplomb onstage, as well. During a performance in Canada, she returned for an encore to sing "When Goodbye Was a Word" with just a piano for accompaniment. A film crew was taping the event, and a camera operator accidentally tripped a cable, cutting off the amplification for the piano. Yearwood continued, performing a cappella. When she finished the song, she received a standing ovation.

At this point, Trisha Yearwood seems ready for any challenge that may come her way.

As with her recordings, Yearwood likes to surprise concert audiences with her song selection by performing lyrics usually associated with male vocalists. For instance, one of her concert favorites has been Merle Haggard's "I Think I'll Just Stay Here and Drink."

DWIGHT YOAKAM

Dwight Yoakam has a country boy's background and a college intellectual's vocabulary, but his story has a Southern California angle. He's a modern-day rebel who fought to revive an old-fashioned musical style. He has accumulated many victories, and he has left some enemies in his wake.

Yoakam roared his way into the country music industry with his first album, *Guitars, Cadillacs, Etc., Etc.*, which was released on Oak Records and funded by $5,000 raised by the singer and his guitarist-producer, Pete Anderson. Reprise Records scooped up the rights to the recordings, then asked Yoakam to add a few songs, and distributed it nationwide.

Both pages: Dwight Yoakam's music is a celebration of traditional Americana. He scored his first hit with a revved-up version of "Honky Tonk Man," a song written in the mid-1950s by Johnny Horton. Yoakam loves Cadillacs and classic cars, and titled his first album *Guitars, Cadillacs, Etc., Etc.*

The first song, a kicking remake of Johnny Horton's "Honky Tonk Man," established Yoakam as a new musical force. However, his outspoken criticism of the Nashville music industry created a less uniform response. Some admired his courage and agreed with his point of view, but others were offended, especially a few leading executives who weren't accustomed to verbal blasts from newcomers.

Yoakam comes from independent stock, however. He was born on October 23, 1956, in Pikeville, a small town in Pike Floyd Hollow in the hills of Kentucky, just a hike from Butcher Hollow, the birthplace of Loretta Lynn. An impoverished, rural area, this part of Kentucky is made up of hard-working, coal-mining people.

While Yoakam was still an infant, his parents, David and Ruth Ann Yoakam, moved 90 miles north to Columbus, Ohio. His father went to work at a Texaco service station, and both parents faced ridicule for their heavy hill-country accents and rural expressions. Their son heard the word "hillbilly" often, used in a derogatory sense. It was a word he wouldn't forget.

Yoakam's torn jeans became one of his trademarks in the late 1980s. He contends that they weren't ripped in order to make a fashion statement—they were just a few favorite pairs that wore out from frequent wear.

On most weekends, his family traveled back to the hills of Kentucky to visit relatives. Yoakam is haunted by vivid memories, both powerful and comforting, of his Kentucky heritage. He remembers his grandfather, Luther Tibbs, rolling on the ground to shake the coal dust from his lungs so he could sit upright without coughing violently. He remembers singing bluegrass and gospel songs on the front porch. He remembers the passionate a cappella singing at the local Church of Christ.

Yoakam wrote his first song at age eight. By 1976, a year out of high

school, he was performing throughout the Ohio Valley. Two years later, he arrived in Nashville, ready to dedicate himself to the style of music he loved. However, he was shocked by the reaction to his music. People recognized his talent, he recalls, but he was told he was "too country"—this in the capital of country music.

Rather than compromise, he moved to Los Angeles. He rented a one-room apartment, slept on a mattress on the floor, and drove an airport freight van by day while singing in the working-class honky tonks of suburban L.A. at night.

Four years later, he met Pete Anderson, an educated young man dedicated to the raw, traditional forms of American music. With Anderson's help, Yoakam's vision became more defined, his attitude more uncompromising.

Before long, other Los Angeles-based, roots-music advocates took an interest in Yoakam. He and his band began opening for such Southern California favorites as Los Lobos, the Blasters, and X. How ironic that this hard-core country singer from a Kentucky hollow found his audience in the punk and roots-rock clubs of one of America's most densely populated regions.

Nashville finally took notice, largely because of the reams of positive press Yoakam was drawing on the West Coast. The singer found favor fast: With Anderson as his producer, Yoakam's first two albums on Reprise Records sold 1.5 million copies in two years. His initial success came right on the heels of *The New York Times* front-

page article that declared the Nashville Sound was dead and a *Time* magazine piece that stated country was in a deep sales slump. Yoakam, along with newcomers Randy Travis and the Judds, helped pump life back into country music at a vital point.

Over the years, Yoakam adjusted his commentary, submitting that his offending words were fueled by his passion for a specific genre of country music. "I would best describe what I'm doing as hillbilly music," he says, "because that encompasses a lot of the forms—bluegrass, honky tonk, western swing, string band music. And when they put electric guitar with bluegrass in the late '40s, and then added some drums and took it to the stage, that's what became hillbilly music. It wasn't really rock 'n' roll. It was its own animal."

Yoakam's music paid tribute to the past, both that of his family and that of country music. Dwight wrote about his coal-mining legacy, about the state highways that people in the rural south took north to find work in industrial centers, and about the mystery and dangers of rural mountain life.

As for his tastes in outside material, he usually looked to the past. Besides the Johnny Horton tune, he has put his spin on classics by Johnny Cash, Buck Owens, Elvis Presley, Stonewall Jackson, Lefty Frizzell, Roger Miller, and Gram Parsons. As for Owens, he helped bring the legendary singer out of retirement. As Owens has related it, the young singer simply showed up at Owens's Bakersfield office unannounced one afternoon. Yoakam then invited his idol to perform with him

that night at a fair. Owens agreed, launching a comeback that would include a number-one duet with Yoakam ("Streets of Bakersfield") and two albums for Capitol Records.

Yoakam hasn't received the number of major awards that his peers have garnered. But he finds solace in sticking to his integrity—and in the sales figures for his records. All of his albums have sold at least a half-million copies.

Behind the scenes, he also displays a devotion to the pioneers and legends of the country music industry. For example, he has developed a close friendship with Minnie Pearl, the country humorist who is one of the cornerstones of the Grand Ole Opry. When Pearl celebrated her 50th anniversary as a member of the Opry, Yoakam sent her 50 roses.

Dwight Yoakam seems a mass of contradictions: He has paved the way for country's new sounds by returning to its traditions; he has criticized the Nashville industry while celebrating its performers; he has become hip by embracing the past. In doing so, he has revitalized country music for a younger generation.

Yoakam has developed friendships with several country music legends, including veteran Grand Ole Opry humorist Minnie Pearl, whom he comforted for several hours during her 1992 hospitalization.

Persistence paid off when Yoakam coaxed his idol, Buck Owens, out of retirement in the late 1980s. Their duet, "Streets of Bakersfield," was a smash.

PHOTO CREDITS: